To my brother Mat, who is very
creative with Origami. Have fun!
Washington D.C. Constitutional
Essay trip. May 1-8, 1988

Your Big Sis,
Danyel

Wings & Things

Wings & Things

Origami That Flies

by Stephen Weiss

with line drawings by Paul Jackson

St. Martin's Press   New York

WINGS & THINGS: ORIGAMI THAT FLIES. Copyright © 1984 by
Stephen Weiss. All rights reserved. Printed in the United States of
America. No part of this book may be used or reproduced in any
manner whatsoever without written permission except in the case of
brief quotations embodied in critical articles or reviews. For
information, address St. Martin's Press, 175 Fifth Avenue, New York,
N.Y. 10010

Design by Laura Hammond Hough

Library of Congress Cataloging in Publication Data

Weiss, Stephen, 1948-
    Wings & things.

    1. Origami.   I. Title.   II. Title: Wings and things.
TT870.W434   1984   736'.982   84-13251
ISBN 0-312-88228-9 (pbk.)

10 9 8 7 6

Acknowledgments

I would like to thank the following:

The origami creators who have allowed me to publish their original models.

Samuel Randlett, Alice Gray, Florence Temko, Paul Jackson, Peter Engel, and Michael LaFosse for their advice and encouragement.

Paul Jackson for his collaboration in producing the drawings and establishing a format.

Arnold Tubis for his help in compiling the bibliography.

Micki Kronowitt and Bettina King for their help in typing and editing the manuscript.

Janice Weiss, Tatiana Venero, and the faculty of the Photography Division of the Visual Arts Department of Palm Beach Junior College, Lake Worth, Florida: Patrick Slatery, Eugene Arant, Edward Kinney, Anita Borody-chuk, and Department Chairman Reuben Hale, for providing assistance in, and facilities for, producing the black-and-white photographs.

My editor, Barbara Anderson, and St. Martin's Press for their assistance, encouragement, and patience.

Janice Weiss and Alice Gray for proofreading.

Contents

Introduction

Since the first recorded paper airplanes, in the notebooks of Leonardo da Vinci, folding paper to make it fly has become one of the world's most popular pastimes.

Safer than hang gliders, quieter than model airplanes, and requiring less room than flying saucers or boomerangs, paper airplanes are a fingertip expression of the freedom of flight.

Designs for more than thirty origami models that fly are presented in this book. There are airplanes, birds, bats, fish, kites, wings, dollar bill gliders, a pentagon, a tube, a maple seed, and even a flying nun. The great variety of shapes and flight patterns is especially appealing. Most people do not expect to see a tube fly across the room, and are delighted (or annoyed) to see paper birds, bats, and fish do the same. No tape, glue, paste, staples, paper clips, or cutouts are needed, and most of the models are made from square or $8^{1}/_{2} \times 11''$ sheets of paper. You will soon find yourself appropriating place mats and advertising fliers for the more sublime purposes of origami.

Paper folding probably originated in China with the invention of paper, but was developed mainly in Japan, over the centuries becoming a part of Japanese culture. The word *origami* is Japanese, meaning "the folding of paper." In the last fifty years origami has progressed from a traditional pastime to a widely practiced creative art form. Today there are active origami societies in many countries around the world.

If origami is new to you, this book will be a good introduction. In fact, the first model is the traditional "paper airplane" known to virtually everyone. It is origami in its simplest form.

Read the first few pages, "How to Use This Book," and you will soon be folding for flight.

NOTE TO PEOPLE IN EDUCATION AND HEALTH PROFESSIONS

Origami is particularly useful in helping to develop
- manual dexterity and fine motor coordination
- the ability to perceive and visualize three-dimensional images and spacial relations
- the ability to follow a series of visual and verbal directions in a precise manner
- the ability to give complex instructions in an accurate manner
- memory
- a sense of accomplishment from producing a tangible result from a series of steps

The fact that these models can fly gives them particularly high interest.

If someone has trouble following the diagrams and/or text, it is helpful to have another person read the verbal instructions aloud while the folder studies the diagrams. The text can also be recorded on tape and played back step by step.

Wings & Things

Origami That Flies

How to Use This Book

FOLLOWING THE INSTRUCTIONS

The models in this book are arranged in an order that helps to build skills and explain techniques as one progresses. For this reason, it is suggested that you start with the first model and work through in sequence.

The folding method for each model is broken down into a series of steps. Each drawing shows two things: the result of the previous steps, and what action must be taken next. If you have trouble with a certain procedure, look ahead to the next drawing, or next few drawings, to see the result. Written directions for each step are also provided and should be used with the drawings. The drawings and text use standard origami notation.

Study the pages which explain the use of the symbols and how to make reverse folds. Refer back to these whenever necessary.

A "valley fold," represented by a series of dashes, indicates a concave crease. A "mountain fold," represented by a series of dots and dashes, indicates a convex crease. Often when a drawing indicates a mountain fold, it is easier to turn the paper over and make the crease as a valley fold. The result is the same.

Since valley folds are more numerous in the drawings than mountain folds, whenever the written directions say "fold," it is assumed to mean "valley fold." Mountain folds are referred to as "mountain folds."

In the text, the terms "upper," "lower," "left," and "right" refer to orientation in relation to the page. The terms "front," "rear," "inner," and "outer" refer to the model itself. "Top" and "bottom" can refer to either the page or the model. The term "near" layer, surface, or flap means that which is uppermost or closest to you. "Far" means that which is away from you.

The first drawing of some models shows crease lines already existing on the paper, dividing it in half diagonally, horizontally, or vertically. These are always assumed to be valley creases and should be put in at the start of the model.

Fold neatly and accurately, making sharp, straight creases. Inaccuracy at the beginning of a model will be amplified at the end. It is usually best to fold on a hard, flat surface. Folding the paper away from you, so that the crease being made is near you, is usually the easiest way to control accuracy.

PAPER

Almost any kind of paper can be used as long as it will hold a crease and won't tear or crack when folded back and forth a few times.

Most of the models in this book use either square or $8^{1/2} \times 11''$ paper.* A few use 3×7 proportion rectangles, which is what dollar bills are. Standard letter-size paper in the United States is $8^{1/2} \times 11''$ and therefore very convenient. Page 19 shows how to cut a square from this or any proportion rectangle.

*In the United States, $8^{1/2} \times 11''$ is the standard size letter paper, but in most of the rest of the world, paper in the proportion $1:\sqrt{2}$ is standard. This comes in various "international sizes." Size A4 is the closest to our $8^{1/2} \times 11''$. Removing $7/8''$ from one end of an A4 size sheet of paper will yield a rectangle of $8^{1/2} \times 11$ proportion.

Rectangles of the proportion $1:\sqrt{2}$, sometimes called "silver" or "true" rectangles, have many interesting geometric characteristics. For example, if a "true" rectangle is divided in half widthwise, the resulting rectangles are each the same proportion ($1:\sqrt{2}$) as the original whole.

Several of the books listed in the bibliography contain models from only this proportion paper.

Origami paper, available at some art supply and craft stores, or from the sources listed at the back of the book, comes in squares which are colored on one side and white on the other. Most origami paper is between 4 and 10″ square and comes in many different colors. Some types have several different hues on the same side in various patterns, and another type, called duo-paper, has a different color on each side.

One way to design origami is to make use of both the colored and uncolored sides of the paper in the finished model. In this book, only the Flying Nun is specifically designed in this way, although some of the other models show a random but pleasing two-tone effect when made with origami paper.

Experiment with different kinds of paper, such as various weights of typing or bond paper, airmail paper, cotton rag paper, tracing paper, art paper, craft paper, plasticized paper, light card, and even thin sheets of plastic like those used for book and report covers.

Some models will work best in a certain size or type of paper. In general, the larger the model is made, the stronger and heavier the paper must be to hold its shape in flight.

Paper-backed metal foil, such as gift wrap, can be made to work well for some models, but it is easily bent out of shape and lacks the self-adjusting springiness of non-foil paper. If models are to be used as decorations, however, foil, especially for airplanes, would be appropriate.

ADJUSTING AND FLYING

At the end of each set of diagrams are suggestions for adjusting and launching the model to achieve the best flights or to make a variety of maneuvers. The last drawings of each set, usually a front view and a hand-held view, show typical wing positions for good flight. The front (or rear) view always shows the position the model assumes at rest, that is, when the body is not held closed. Each model must be adjusted individually as it is tested because slight variations made when folding, the type and size of paper, and even weather conditions, all affect performance. As a general rule, check that leading edges are well creased and straight, wings are symmetrically shaped and evenly raised on both sides, and tail fins and flaps are straight and even. After a while, you will get a feel for what things to do to improve or change flight.

Don't be discouraged if a model doesn't turn out well at first. It takes practice to become familiar with the procedures and the manipulation of the paper. If a model will not fly no matter what you do, it is best to start over with a new piece of paper, perhaps of a different size or type.

Certain models, such as the Flying Bats, Flying Fish, Maple Seed, and Seagull, lend themselves to being launched from a height, such as a second- or third-story balcony, or launched upward into calm air or a light breeze, where they may catch the wind and stay airborne for quite some time.

Although aerodynamic principles are not described in this book (that task being left to other publications devoted to the subject), it is worth noting that the aerodynamic and physical principles involved in some of the models are quite unusual. For example, the Astro Tube makes use of gyroscopic motion, gyroscopic precession, weathervaning, and planing. The flying saucer–like Penta-Flinger uses some of these same effects although differently (as does the boomerang).

Inherent to origami is a type of wing design, shown in a number of models, that has enhanced anti-stall characteristics. The basic factor is a wing under-surface which is sharply recessed at some point behind the leading edge, continuing so to the trailing edge. This was first discovered (and patented) by Richard Kline and Floyd Fogleman after Kline noticed the effect in a paper airplane he had designed (see Bibliography).

Besides demonstrating aerodynamics, making origami that flies is a lot of fun. The creative process is part of the total enjoyment of origami, and you are encouraged to apply what you learn here to invent your own original designs.

SYMBOLS

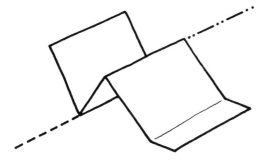

- – – – – – – – – • Valley fold—fold upward or toward you

- •–•—••—••—••–• • Mountain fold—fold backward or away from you

- ————————— • Existing crease—the result of a previous fold

- ••••••••••••••••••• • X-ray view (or line projection)—something that happens inside where you can't see it

- ——————→ • Move the paper in this direction

- ——————▷ • Fold back this way

- ⟷ • Fold and unfold

- ⇉ • Unfold, open out

- ⇨ • Push in or apply pressure

- ⇨ • The next drawing is larger

- ↺↻ • Raise or lower wings to flying position

- •——————→• • Fold, laying one dot on top of the other

- ⌢⌢→ • Fold over and over

- ⟲→ • Turn the model over

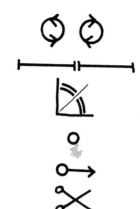

- Rotate the model (counterclockwise or clockwise)

- These distances are equal

- These angles are equal

- Hold here

- Hold here and pull

- Cut here

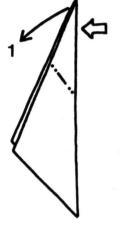

INSIDE REVERSE FOLD

1–3   Part of an edge, which is a mountain fold, is pushed down between the near and far layers of the paper. The edge becomes a valley fold.

1a–1b   It is sometimes helpful to precrease the paper where you want the reverse fold to be, and then reverse fold along those creases.

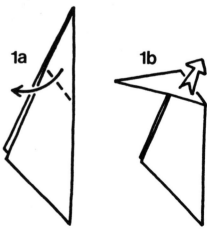

OUTSIDE REVERSE FOLD

1–3   The near and far layers of the paper are spread apart and wrapped around the outside of the model. The edge which was a valley fold becomes a mountain fold.

1a–1b   Again, it is sometimes easier to precrease the paper before making the reverse fold.

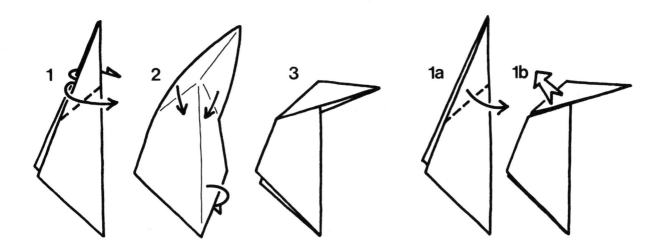

HOW TO MAKE A SQUARE FROM A RECTANGLE

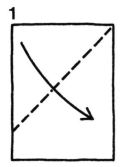
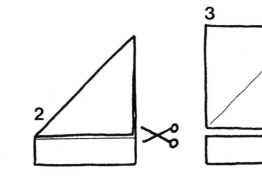

1. Simple Dart

Traditional.

Use an 8½ × 11″ sheet of paper. Fold the paper in half vertically (lengthwise) and then unfold it.

1. Fold the top corners in to the vertical center line so that each half of the top edge lies along the center line.
2. Bring the folded edges in to lie along the vertical center line.

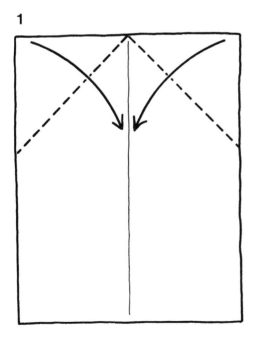

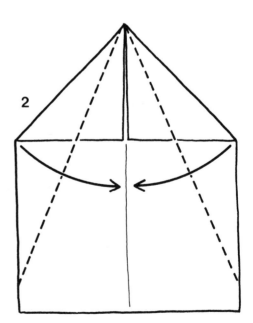

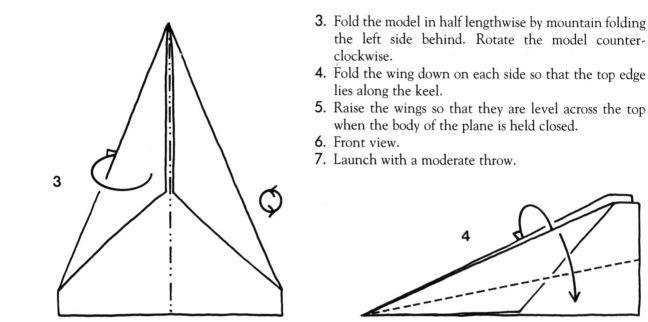

3. Fold the model in half lengthwise by mountain folding the left side behind. Rotate the model counter-clockwise.
4. Fold the wing down on each side so that the top edge lies along the keel.
5. Raise the wings so that they are level across the top when the body of the plane is held closed.
6. Front view.
7. Launch with a moderate throw.

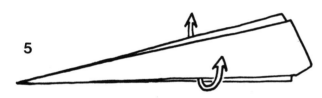

6

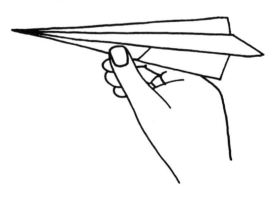

2. Blackboard Bomber

Designed by George Jarschauer.
Based on a model by Eiji Nakamura.

Use an 8½ × 11″ sheet of paper.
1. Mountain fold the paper in half vertically. Unfold.
2. Fold the top edges to the vertical center line.
3. (The drawing is larger.) Fold the triangular top section down at its base.

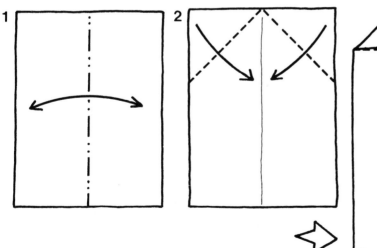

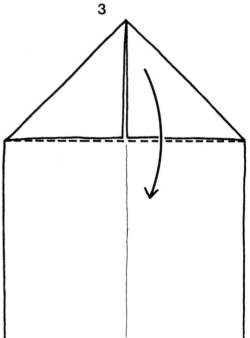

4

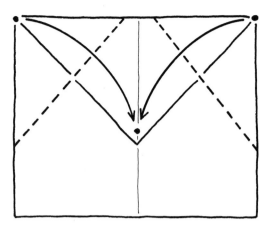

5

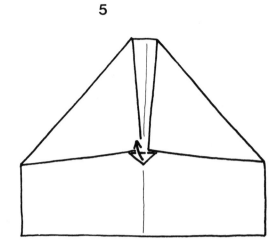

6

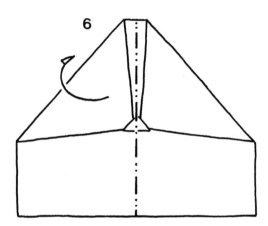

7

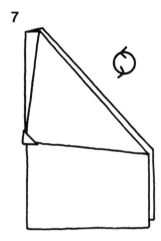

4. Fold the upper corners down to a point on the vertical center line about ½" above the bottom point of the triangle.
5. Fold the small triangular tip up over the two corners. This locks the underbody together.
6. Fold the model in half by mountain folding the left side behind.
7. Rotate the model counterclockwise.

8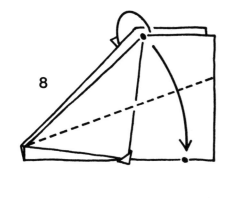

9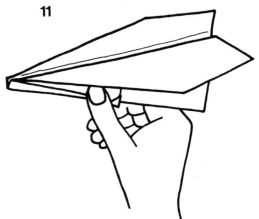

10

11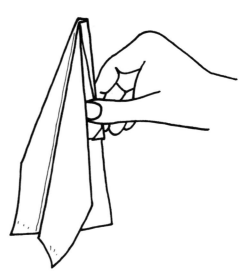

8. Starting from the top of the blunted nose, fold the wing down on each side so that the points shown on wing and keel touch.
9. Raise the wings so that they are level across the top when the body of the plane is held closed.
10. Front view.
11. Launch with a moderate throw. If the plane tends to go down, insert a finger inside the wings to make them slightly convex.
12. To make the plane loop, curl the rear corners of the wings up slightly and launch upward as shown. The plane will loop up and away. The more the corners are curled, the smaller the loop will be.

12

3. Floater

Designed by Stephen Weiss.

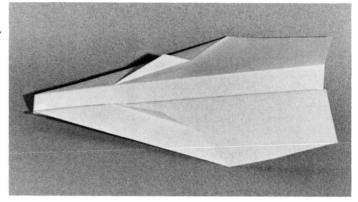

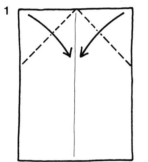

Use an $8^{1/2} \times 11''$ sheet of paper.

1. Fold the top edges in to the vertical center line.
2. Bring the folded edges in on each side to a position $2/3$ of the distance to the center line.
3. Bring the top point down to where the turned-in corners meet at the center, and pinch to mark the halfway point. Return the top point to its original position. Turn the model over.
4. (The drawing is larger.) Fold the tip down to the halfway point marked in step 3.

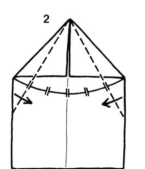

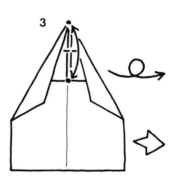

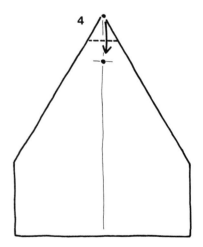

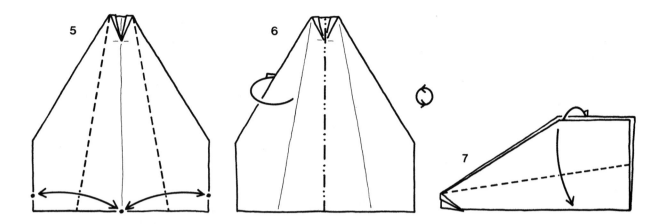

5. Fold the outer edges to the center of the bottom edge as shown. Unfold.

6. Fold the model in half by mountain folding the left side behind. Rotate the model counterclockwise.

7. Fold the wing down on each side along the creases made in step 5.

8. Fold a flap down on each side so that the crease is parallel to the lower front edge of the wing.

9. Raise the wings so that they are level across the top when the body of the plane is held closed. Raise the flaps perpendicular to the wings.

10. Front view.

11. Launch with a gentle or moderate throw. The plane will slow at the end of its flight and float gently down. If it slows, stalls, and dives, lower the wings slightly until the plane appears to hang in the air during flight.

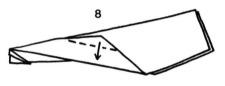

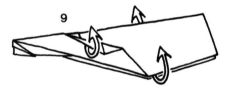

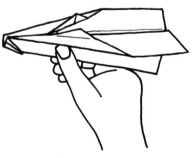

4. SST

Designed by Stephen Weiss.

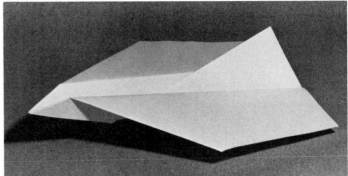

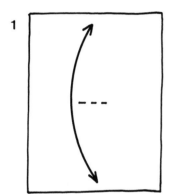

1

Use an 8½ × 11″ sheet of paper.
1. Bring the top and bottom edges together and pinch, to mark the center point.
2. Fold the bottom edge up to the center.
3. Mountain fold the model in half vertically. Unfold.
4. (The drawing is larger.) Fold the bottom edges to the vertical center line.

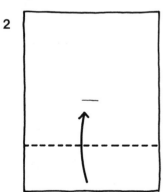

2

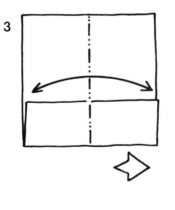

3

4

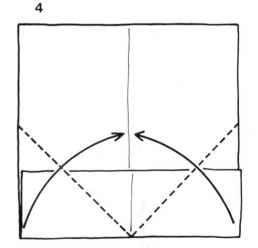

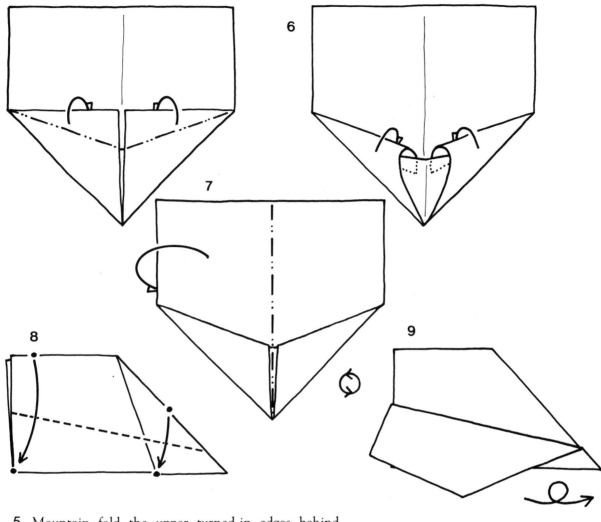

5. Mountain fold the upper turned-in edges behind, tucking them under the layer below.
6. Step 5 in progress.
7. Fold the model in half vertically, by mountain folding the left side behind. Rotate the model counter-clockwise.
8. Fold the upper edges of the near wing to touch the points shown on the bottom edge of the keel.
9. Turn the model over.
10. Fold the keel up from the rear of the thick layer to the rear edge where the wing is folded down.

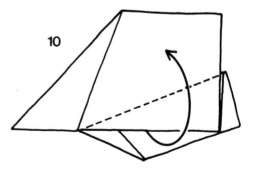

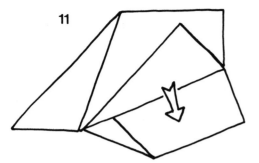

11

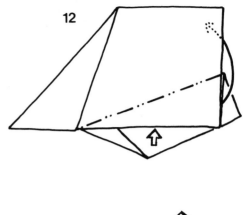

12

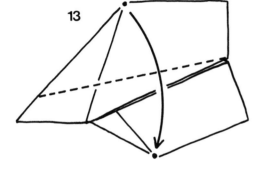

13

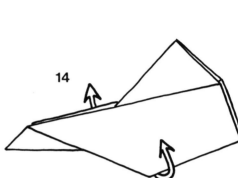

14

15

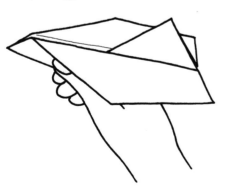

16

11. Unfold the keel back down.
12. Inside reverse fold the keel up along the creases made in steps 10 and 11. This will be the tail fin.
13. Fold the near wing down so that its edges match the wing behind.
14. Raise the wings so that they are level across the top when the body of the plane is held closed.
15. Front view.
16. Launch with a gentle to moderate throw. The plane should fly very smoothly. If it tends to fly downward, brush the rear corners upward very slightly.

5. Dollar Bill Glider I

Designed by Stephen Weiss.
Idea for step 1 by George Rhoads.

Use a new dollar bill or any 3 × 7 proportion rectangle of paper.

1. Fold the bottom left corner to the top right corner. Rotate the model counterclockwise.
2. Fold the model in half vertically. Unfold. Turn the model over.

1

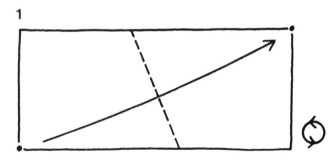

2

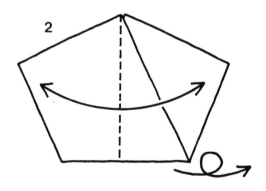

3

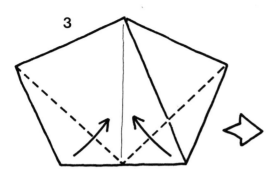

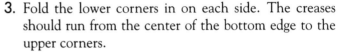

4

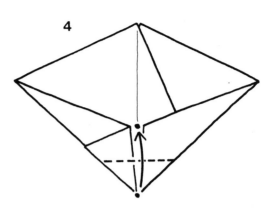

5

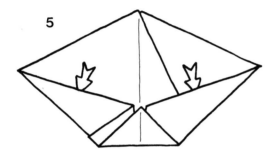

3. Fold the lower corners in on each side. The creases should run from the center of the bottom edge to the upper corners.
4. (The drawing is larger.) Fold the bottom point up to lie between the turned-in corners.
5. Push your thumbs between the top and bottom layers of the wings to make them convex.
6. Mountain fold the glider along the center line to raise the wings. Turn the model over.
7. Front view.
8. Hold the glider lightly by the tail and release with a gentle forward push. If the glider turns too much, be sure the wings are evenly shaped.

6

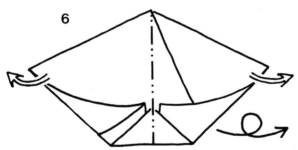

7

8

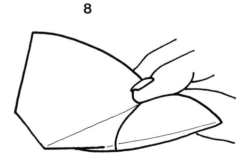

6. Astro Tube

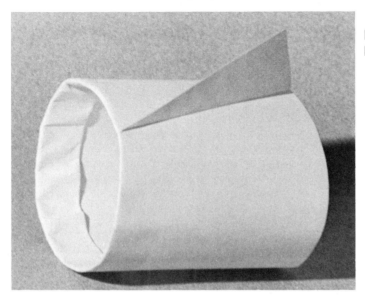

Designed by Stephen Weiss.
Principles and features adapted from
    various sources (including a tube with fin
    by Akira Yoshizawa).

Use an 8½ × 11" sheet of paper.
   1. Fold up ⅓ of the paper.
   2. Fold the doubled section in half.

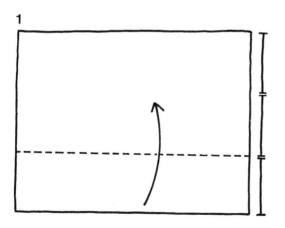

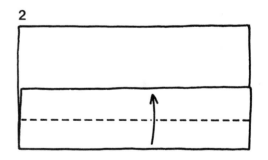

3

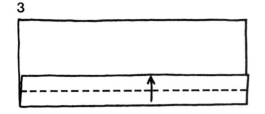

4

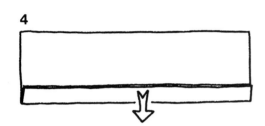

5

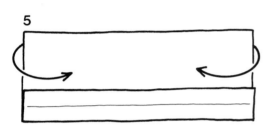

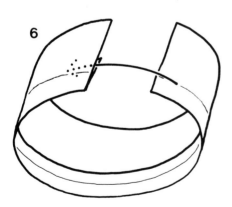

6

7

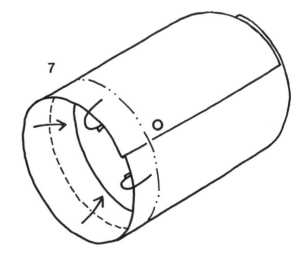

3. Fold the section in half once more and crease well.
4. Unfold.
5. Curve the ends together to form a tube.
6. (The drawing is larger.) Insert the right end inside the left end between the single outer layer and the doubled layers. Overlap the ends about 1½″. For a left-handed tube, insert the left end inside the right end.
7. Hold the tube at the seam with one hand where shown by the circle and turn the rim in along the pre-crease made in steps 3 and 4. Start turning in at the seam and roll the rim under, moving around the circumference in a circular manner. Then round out the rim.

Note to Magicians:
The Astro Tube can be used as a clever way of vanishing a silk handkerchief in the typical manner used to vanish cigarettes. Pre-fold the tube and unfold it. Quickly refold the tube on stage, stuff the handkerchief in, vanish it, and show the tube to be empty. Then toss the tube into the audience for inspection. (The idea for this routine is by Barry Gibbs.)

8. Fold the fin to the left and then raise it up perpendicular to the tube. Be careful not to tear the paper at the front. For the left-handed version, the fin will angle the other way.

9. Front view.

10. Hold the tube near the rim from above between the thumb and fingers. The rim end should be forward, with the fin on the bottom. Throw the tube underhanded, letting it spin off the fingers as it is released. The tube will float through the air, spinning as it goes.

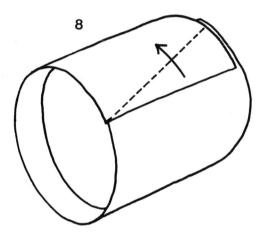

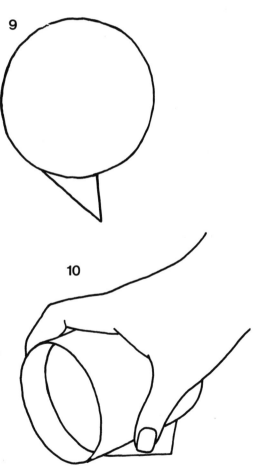

The Astro Tube works best if made from stiff or heavy paper, or even light card. For smaller children, use a smaller rectangle, or a square made from an 8½ × 11" sheet (8½ × 8½"). By applying the same procedure to a new dollar bill, you can make a small ring-like version of the tube.

The Astro Tube can also be thrown overhand, like a football, as well as underhand, but the joining of the ends and direction of the fin must be reversed as when changing for right or left hand throws in steps 6 and 8.

7. Space Wing

Designed by Stephen Weiss.

Use a square of paper, preferably at least 8″ a side.
1. Mountain fold the paper in half vertically. Unfold.
2. Fold the paper in half horizontally. Unfold.
3. Fold the bottom edge up to the horizontal center line.

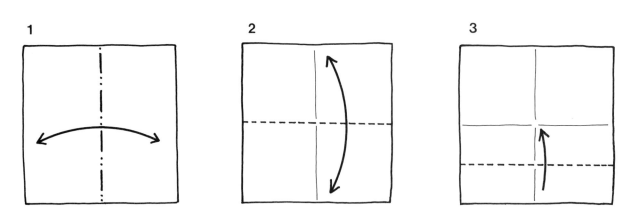

4

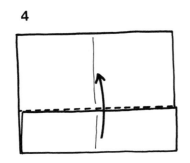

5

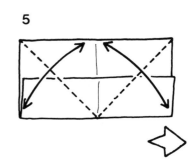

6

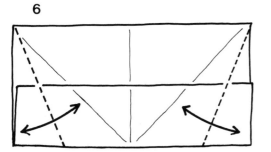

7

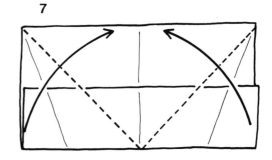

8

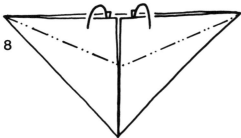

9

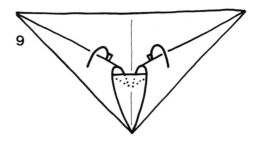

4. Fold the doubled paper up at the horizontal line.
5. Fold the lower edges to the vertical center line. Unfold.
6. (The drawing is larger.) Fold the ends to the diagonal creases on each side. Unfold.
7. Fold the lower edges to the vertical center line again.
8. Mountain fold the upper edges behind along the creases made in step 6. Tuck the edges under the layer below.
9. Step 8 in progress.
10. Fold the bottom point up to the point where the upper folded edges meet. Pinch to mark and unfold.

10

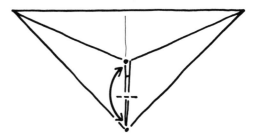

11

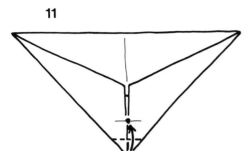

12

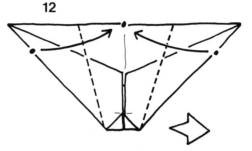

13

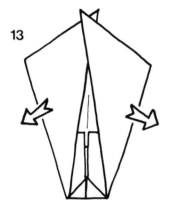

14

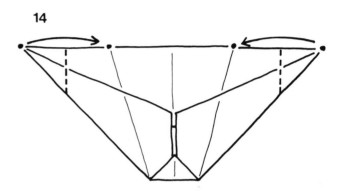

15

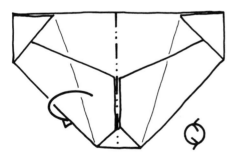

11. Fold the bottom point up to the mark on the center line made in step 10.
12. Fold the left and right edges in from each side of the blunted nose so that they cross the center of the top (or rear) edge.
13. (The drawing is larger.) Unfold.
14. Fold the left and right corners in to touch the point on each side where the crease intersects the top edge.
15. Fold the model in half by mountain folding the left side behind. Rotate the model counterclockwise.

16

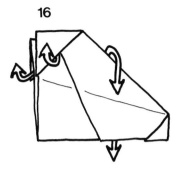

17

18

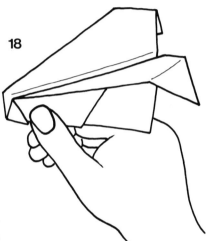

16. Fold the wings down along the creases made in step 12 so that they are level. Unfold the wing tips down perpendicular to the wings.

17. Front view.

18. Hold as shown. The Space Wing can be launched with a gentle or hard throw. The model should fly very straight and level. If it doesn't, make sure the leading edges are well creased, including the flaps, and the wings are level when the model is held loosely. The flaps should be straight down. Sometimes making the top surface of each wing slightly convex or concave helps. This depends on the size and type of paper used.

8. Sky Cruiser

Designed by Michael LaFosse.

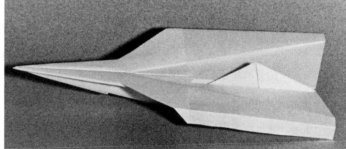

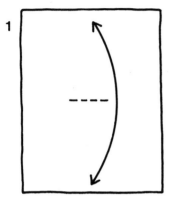

Use an 8½ × 11″ sheet of paper.
1. Bring the top and bottom edges together and pinch to mark the center point.
2. Fold the bottom edge up to the center.
3. Turn the model over.
4. Fold the model in half vertically. Unfold.
5. Fold the bottom edges to the center line.

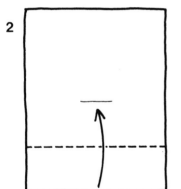

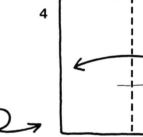

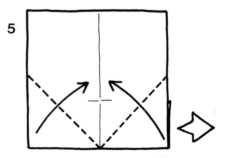

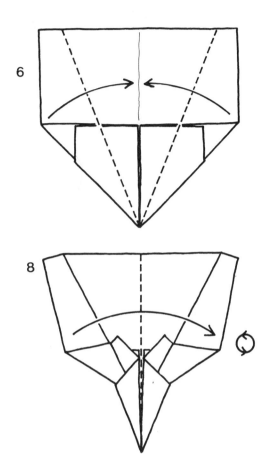

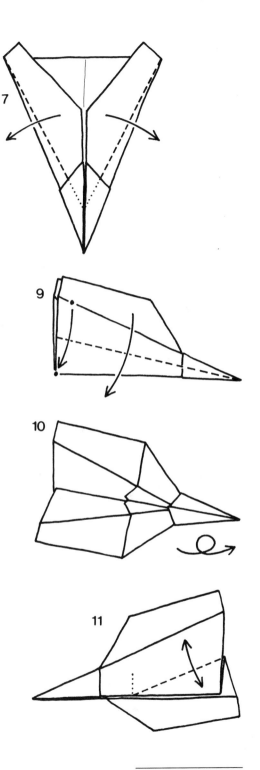

6. (The drawing is larger.) Fold the lower edges in to the center line.

7. Fold the middle layer on each side to the outside. To do this, start folding from the outer top corner and move the edge that lies along the center line under the layer of the nose to the outside as far as it will go.

8. Fold the model in half vertically, bringing the left side to the right side. Rotate the model counterclockwise.

9. Fold down the near wing so that the edge marked lines up with the keel.

10. Turn the model over.

11. Fold the keel up from the inner layer (X-ray line) to the rear edge where the wing is folded down. Unfold.

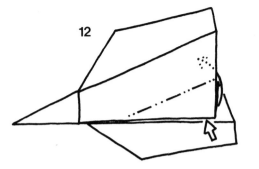

12. Inside reverse fold the keel up along the creases made in step 11. This will be the tail fin.
13. Fold the near wing down so that its edges match the wing behind.
14. Fold the rear edges of the tail fin over, tucking them as far down as they will go.
15. Mountain fold behind the outer edge of the wing so that the fold is parallel to the edge and divides the outermost rear edge in half. Repeat behind on the other wing.
16. Raise the wings so they are level across the top. The side flaps should be straight down.
17. Front view.
18. Launch with a moderate throw.

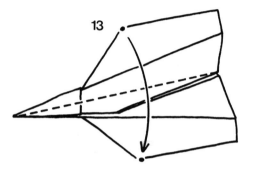

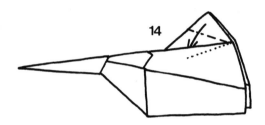

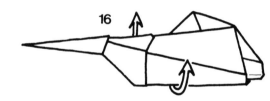

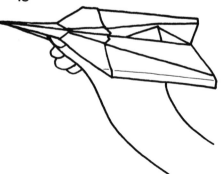

9. Flying Bat I

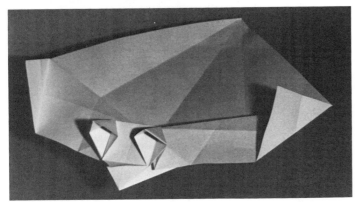

Designed by Stephen Weiss.

Use a square of paper, preferably black or brown. If origami paper is used, the colored side should be up. This model works best made from paper 3 to 6″ a side. Fold the square in half diagonally and unfold it.

1. Fold the lower edges to the center line.
2. Mountain fold the top triangle behind.
3. Unfold the paper completely.
4. (The drawing is larger.) Fold the upper left edge in, so that the top corner touches the point where the crease lines intersect the upper right edge.
5. Unfold.

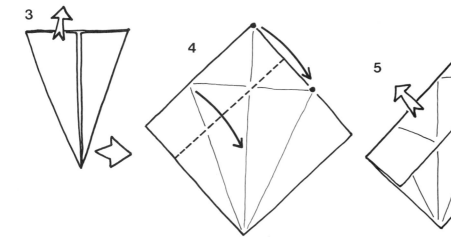

6. Fold the upper right edge in so that the top corner touches the point where the crease lines intersect the upper left edge.
7. Unfold.
8. Fold the left and right upper sides in at the same time. A flap will form at the top. Squash this flap down along existing creases.
9. Step 8 in progress.
10. Fold the bottom of the small square to the top.
11. (The drawing is larger.) Fold the inner edge on each side to the front folded edge.
12. Unfold.

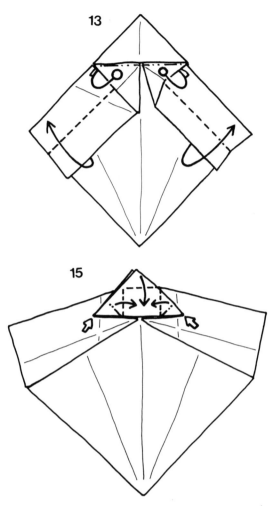

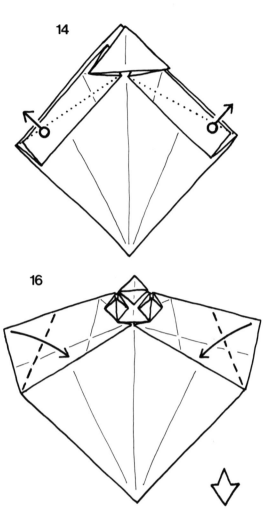

13. Refold the inner edges to the front edges, pushing the triangular sections near the center under the large triangle.

14. Grasp the nearest layer of the left corner and swivel the paper clockwise as far as possible. Flatten as in step 15. Repeat this symmetrically on the right side.

15. Squash down each ear with two layers on the outer side and one layer on the inner side. Fold the nose back.

16. Fold the short outer edges to the folded edges.

17. Enlarged view of the head. Open the ears and fold the nose up.

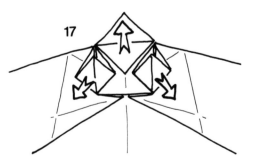

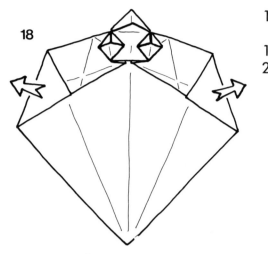

18

19

18. Unfold the corner flaps straight up perpendicular to the rear edges of the body.
19. Front view.
20. Hold the Flying Bat lightly at the rear and drop it forward with a gentle motion. The bat should float slowly and smoothly. If it wobbles and stalls, increase the "valley" of the center crease. If the bat goes out and somersaults, flatten the center crease. Try dropping the bat from a second story, inside or outside.

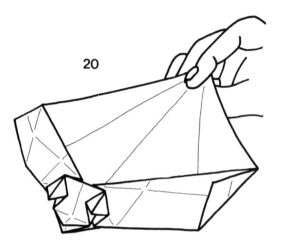

20

10. Origami Kite

Collected and adapted by Michelle Cumbo and Michael Siegel.

You will need a 10″ square of paper, a 6″ square of paper, and kite string.

THE TAIL (6″ SQUARE)

1. Cut the square spirally, as shown.
2. Enlarged view of center. Fold the last segment in half vertically.
3. Fold it in half again.
4. Fold in half again, producing a narrow prong.

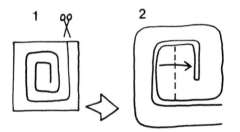

THE KITE (10″ SQUARE)

Fold the square in half diagonally and unfold it.
1. Fold the upper edges to the center line.
2. Fold the bottom turned-in edges to the outer folded edges.
3. Punch small holes for the string and tail where shown. These can be reinforced with plastic adhesive rings, if desired.
4. & 5. Attach the kite string through one of the upper holes with a simple overhand knot. Then attach a short piece of string through the other upper hole. Tie the short string to the long string where shown.

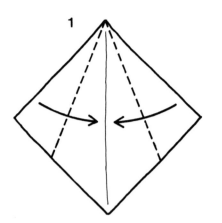

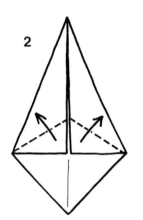

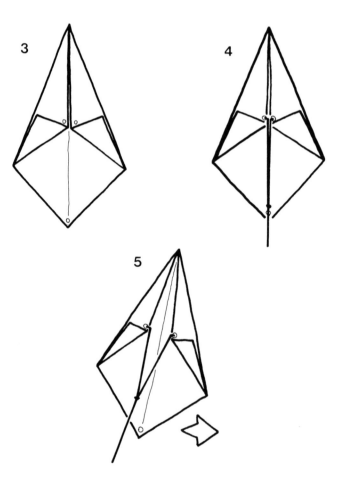

6. Enlarged view of bottom. Insert the prong of the tail through the bottom hole of the kite from the back.
7. Twist the protruding prong into a compact shape, to prevent the tail from slipping out.
8. Result.
9. Hold the string a foot or two from the kite and let the wind carry it away. If the wind is very light, run into it.

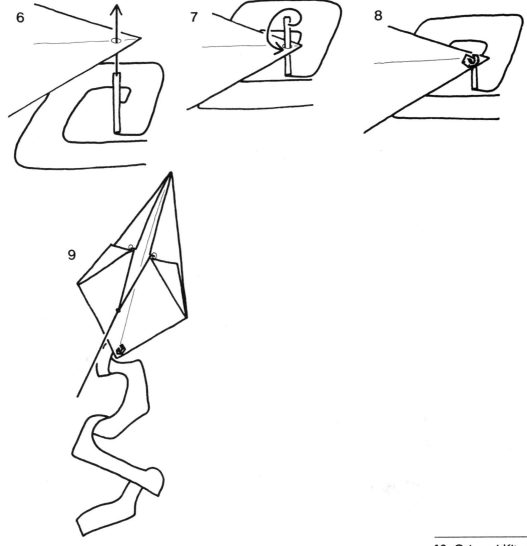

11. Bat Kite

Designed by Stephen Weiss.

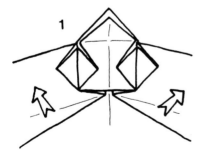

Make the Flying Bat I, 9, using a 10″ square of paper. Make the tail of the Origami Kite, 10, using a 6″ square of paper.

1. Spread apart the back of the head of the Flying Bat I.

2. Punch a small hole under the head near the tip of the jaw.
3. Insert the kite string through the hole from the underside of the bat and tie it around a small rectangle of cardboard. Reclose the head.
4. Punch a small hole near the rear corner of the bat. Insert the prong of the tail through the hole from the underside of the bat. Twist the protruding prong to keep the tail from slipping out. Sometimes shortening the tail will help the kite fly better.

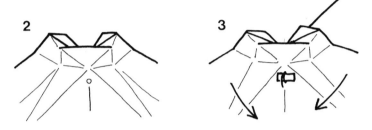

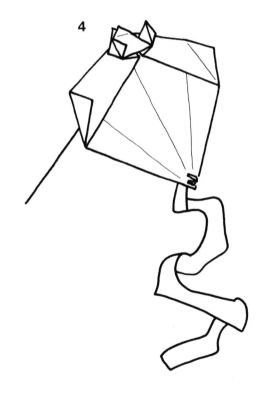

12. Dollar Bill Glider II

Designed by Stephen Weiss.

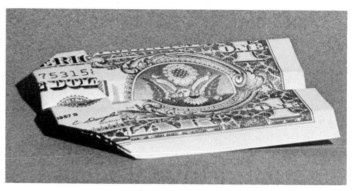

Use a new dollar bill or any 3 × 7 proportion rectangle of paper. 4³/₄ × 11″ works well for this model.

1. Fold the left edges in to the horizontal center line.
2. Fold the triangular section in at its base. Unfold.
3. Fold the left end up so that the crease at the base of the triangle lies along the upper edge.
4. Unfold.

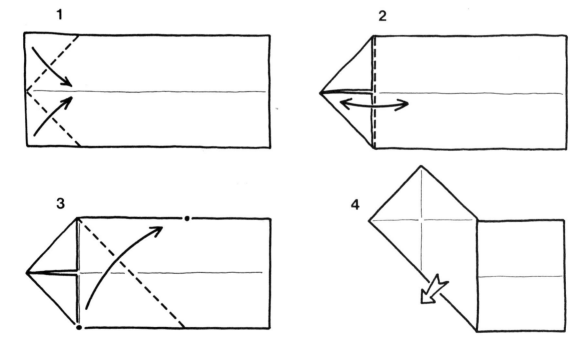

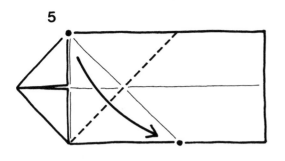

5

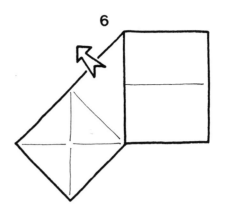

6

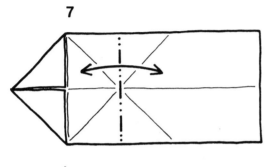

7

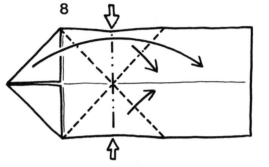

8

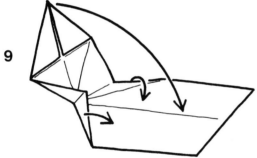

9

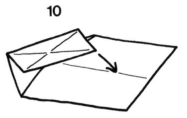

10

5. Fold the left end down so that the crease at the base of the triangle lies along the lower edge.
6. Unfold.
7. Make a vertical mountain fold through the intersection of the diagonal creases.
8. Fold the left end toward the right while pressing in the sides between the diagonal creases.
9. Step 8 in progress.
10. Nearly completed.

11

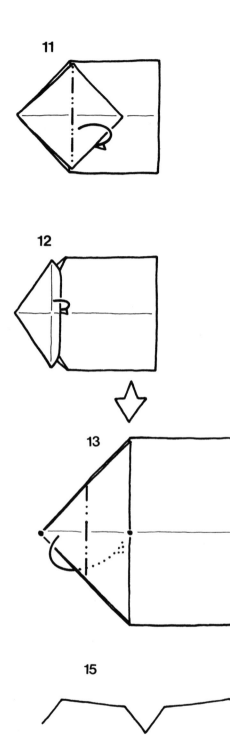

11. Mountain fold the triangular section behind so that it goes between the bottom layer and the turned-in sides.
12. Step 11 in progress.
13. (The drawing is larger.) Mountain fold the tip behind to the point shown.
14. Form the keel and fold down the sides of the wings as shown. The keel and wing flaps are $\frac{1}{8}$ the width of the glider (when flat).
15. Front view.
16. Launch with a gentle to moderate throw with as little distortion to the front view as possible.

12

13

14

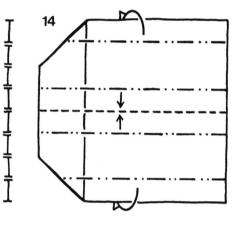

15

16

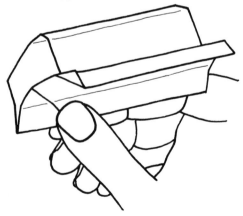

13. Dollar Bill Glider III

Designed by Stephen Weiss.

Use a new dollar bill or any 3 × 7 proportion rectangle of paper.

1. Fold the left side up so that the horizontal and vertical mid-line creases match up.
2. Fold the model in half. Unfold.
3. (The drawing is larger.) Fold the outer front edges to the inner rear edges.

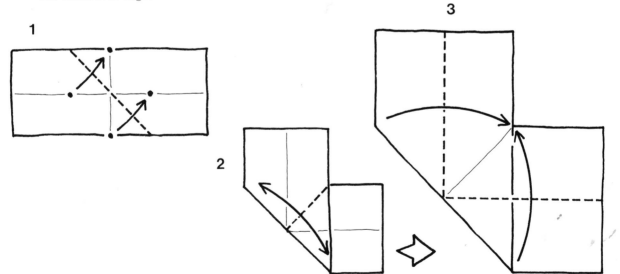

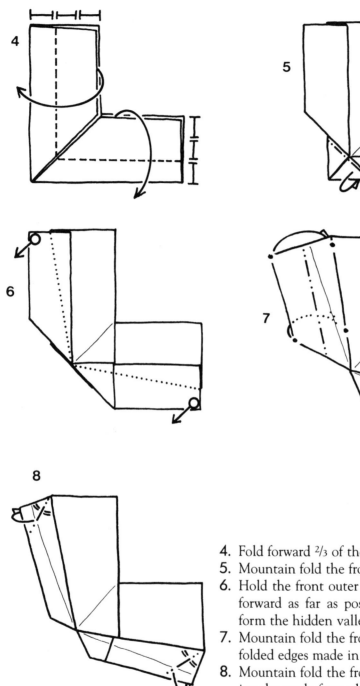

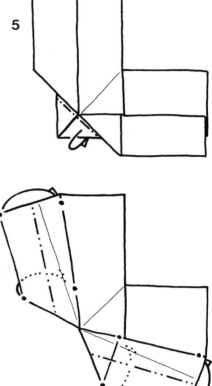

4. Fold forward ²/₃ of the near layer on each side.
5. Mountain fold the front triangle behind.
6. Hold the front outer corners as shown and pull them forward as far as possible. The paper will swivel to form the hidden valley folds (X-ray lines).
7. Mountain fold the front edges behind to lie along the folded edges made in step 6.
8. Mountain fold the front outer corners behind, bisecting the angle formed by the folded and outer edges.

9

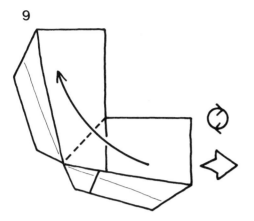

10

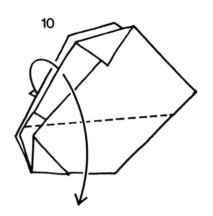

11

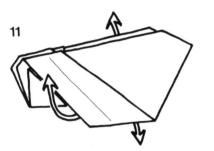

12

13

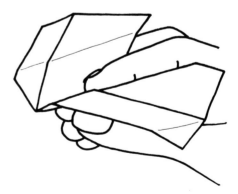

9. Fold the model in half. Rotate it clockwise.
10. (The drawing is larger.) Fold the wing down on each side so that the front edge lies along the edge of the triangle.
11. Raise the wings to a level position and unfold the corner flaps straight down.
12. Front view.
13. Hold as shown and release with a gentle forward push.

14. Tumble Wing

Designed by Kōsho Uchiyama.

Use a square of paper.
1. Fold the top and bottom corners to the center.
2. Bring the top and bottom folded edges to the center line.
3. Make a vertical mountain crease in the center. Then make the two diagonal valley creases by lining up the vertical and horizontal center lines.
4. (The drawing is larger.) Fold the left side to the right side, pushing in the paper between the diagonal creases.
5. Step 4 in progress.

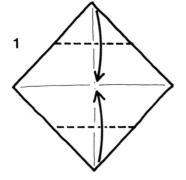

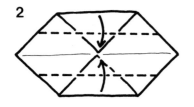

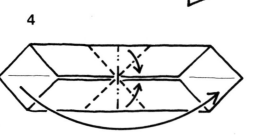

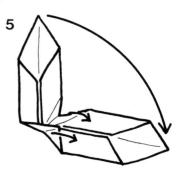

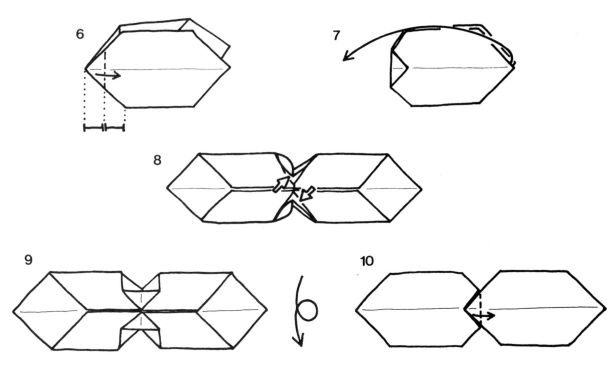

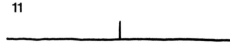

6. Fold the left corner over so that the tip lies between the top and bottom corners of the left end.
7. Swing the near layer to the left, keeping the left corner folded against it.
8. Squash down the reverse folded paper at the center, top, and bottom. Flatten it symmetrically.
9. Result. Turn the model over top to bottom.
10. Crease the center tab to the right and then raise it straight up.
11. Front view.
12. Hold the Tumble Wing as shown and release it with a slight forward push. It will rotate backwards along its lateral axis as it travels forward. (The same effect can be achieved simply by folding a new dollar bill in half lengthwise and launching in a similar manner.)

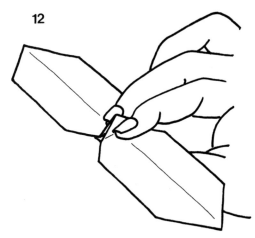

15. Flapping Bird

Designed by Stephen Weiss.

1

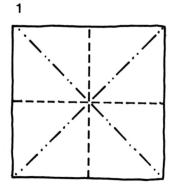

This bird does not fly, but will flap its wings when the tail is pulled.

Use a square of paper.
1. Put in the valley and mountain creases shown which divide the paper in half four ways.
2. Fold the top to the bottom.
3. Hold both layers on each side where indicated by the circles and bring your hands together. The paper will form into four flaps.
4. (The drawing is larger.) Flatten the model with two flaps on each side. In origami this is called a "preliminary fold."

2

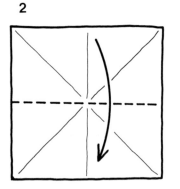

3

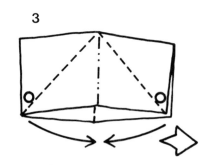

4

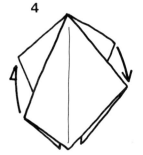

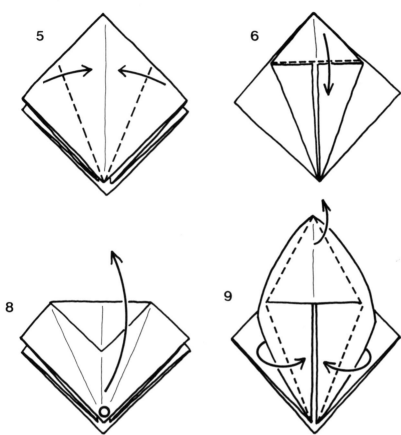

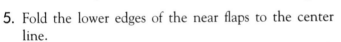

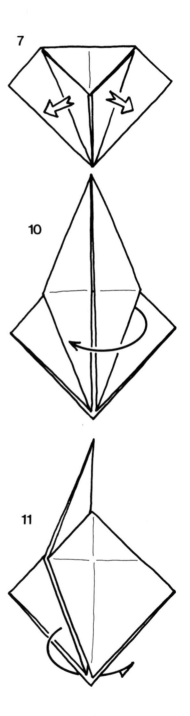

5. Fold the lower edges of the near flaps to the center line.

6. Fold the top triangular section down over the turned-in edges.

7. Pull out the flaps from under the triangular section.

8. Lift the single near layer and swing it upward. The triangular section will go up with it.

9. As you continue lifting, turn the sides in along the existing creases, letting the edges meet along the center line. The direction of the upper creases must be changed from valley to mountain, as viewed from the outside of the flap.

10. Complete. This is called a "petal fold." Swing the right half of the petal fold to the left.

11. Swing the left side of the far flap to the right, behind.

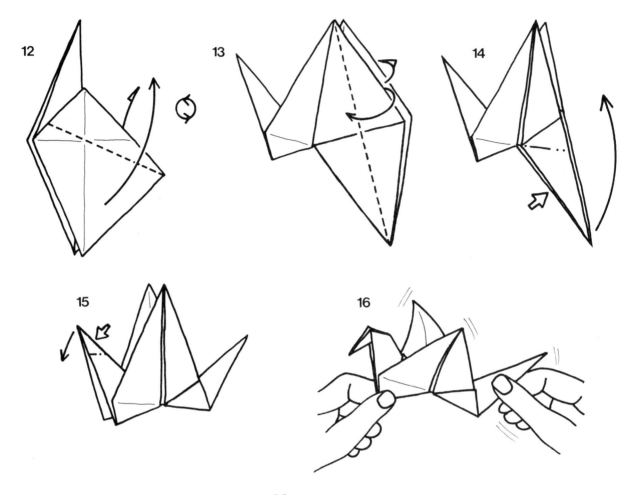

12. Fold each wing up from the right corner as far as the paper in the center will allow. The front edges at the chest should be even. Rotate the model counterclockwise.

13. Fold the right edges to the center edges. They should line up exactly. Repeat behind.

14. Inside reverse fold the tail up so that its top edge is in line with the top edge of the layer at its base.

15. Inside reverse fold the head down.

16. Hold the chest with one hand and pull the tail gently in and out with the other hand to make the wings flap. Curving the wings down will help start the action if it is resistant at first.

16. Flying Bird

Designed by Stephen Weiss.

Use a square of paper at least 6″ a side.

1. Put in the valley and mountain creases shown which divide the paper in half four ways.
2. Fold the top half down.
3. Hold both layers on each side where indicated by the circles and bring your hands together. The paper will form into four flaps.
4. (The drawing is larger.) Flatten the model with two flaps on each side. In origami this is known as a "waterbomb base." A waterbomb base is a preliminary fold turned inside out. (See Flapping Bird, 15.)

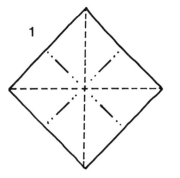

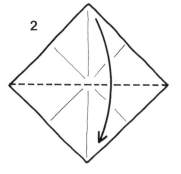

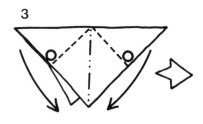

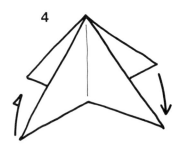

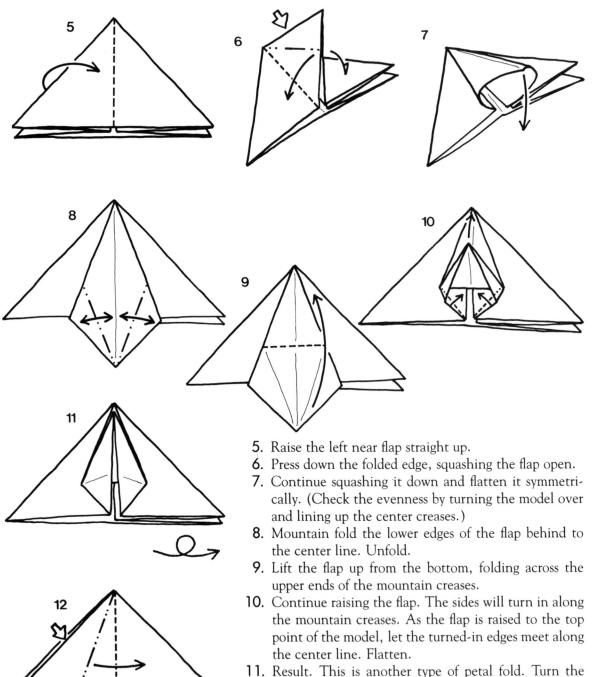

5. Raise the left near flap straight up.
6. Press down the folded edge, squashing the flap open.
7. Continue squashing it down and flatten it symmetrically. (Check the evenness by turning the model over and lining up the center creases.)
8. Mountain fold the lower edges of the flap behind to the center line. Unfold.
9. Lift the flap up from the bottom, folding across the upper ends of the mountain creases.
10. Continue raising the flap. The sides will turn in along the mountain creases. As the flap is raised to the top point of the model, let the turned-in edges meet along the center line. Flatten.
11. Result. This is another type of petal fold. Turn the model over.
12. Squash down the left near flap as in steps 5–7.

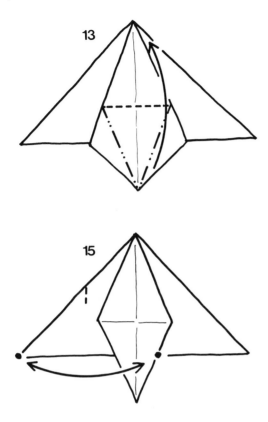

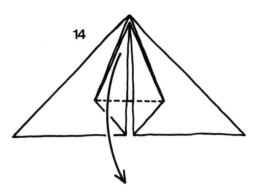

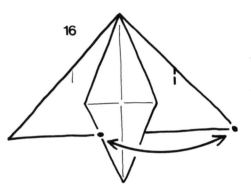

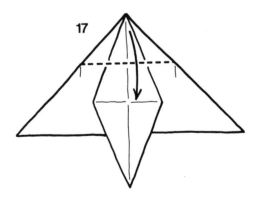

13. Petal fold the flap as in steps 8–11.
14. Swing the flap down.
15. Bring the lower left corner to touch the point of intersection of the lower right edge of the flap and the bottom edge of the model. Make a pinch mark on the upper left edge and return the corner.
16. Bring the lower right corner to touch the point of intersection of the lower left edge of the flap and the bottom edge of the model. Make a pinch mark on the upper right edge and return the corner.
17. Fold down the top of the model so that the fold connects the pinch marks where they touch the left and right edges.

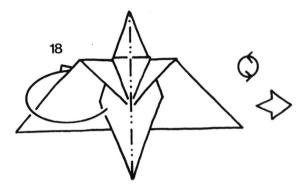

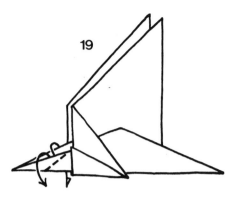

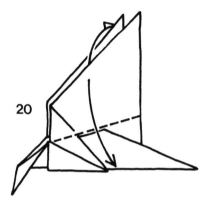

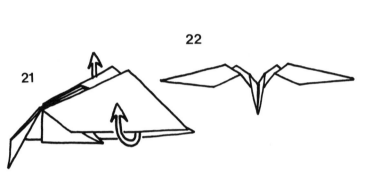

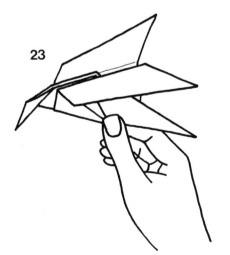

18. Fold the model in half by mountain folding the left side behind. Rotate the model counterclockwise.
19. (The drawing is larger.) Outside reverse fold the head down.
20. Fold down the wing on each side along the front upper edge of the body. The outer edge of each wing will lie along the bottom edge of the model.
21. Raise the wings.
22. Front view.
23. Launch with a gentle to moderate throw. Be sure the leading edges of the wings are well creased and even, and the head is straight. Adjust wing elevation for best flight.

17. Soaring Eagle

Designed by Stephen Weiss.

Use a square of paper.

1. First make separately the long valley creases by bringing the lower edges to the horizontal center line. Then
   fold them both in at the same time. A small flap will
   form in the center. Pinch the flap together and lay it
   to the left. This type of fold is known as a "rabbit ear."

2. Crease the flap to the right, bring it back up, and then
   flatten it, squashing it down symmetrically.

3. Result.

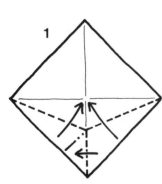

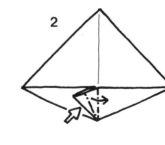

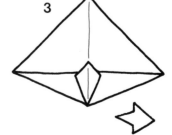

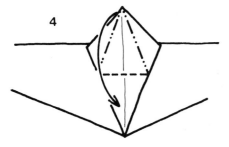

4

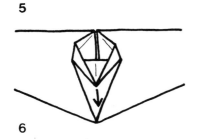

5

6

4. Enlarged view of the flap. Petal fold the flap, bringing the tip to the bottom of the model. (See steps 8–10 of the Flying Bird, 16.)
5. Petal fold in progress.
6. Complete.
7. Mountain fold the bottom of the model behind, pivoting the paper at the widest part of the flap.
8. Starting on the bottom from the widest points of the flap, fold the lower edge up on each side so that the outer edges are even.
9. (The drawing is larger.) Fold the model in half, left to right. Rotate it clockwise.
10. Fold the near surface up from the wide point of the front flap to the upper rear corner of the paper behind. Allow the paper behind to rotate to the outside. Repeat on the other side.
11. Raise the wings.

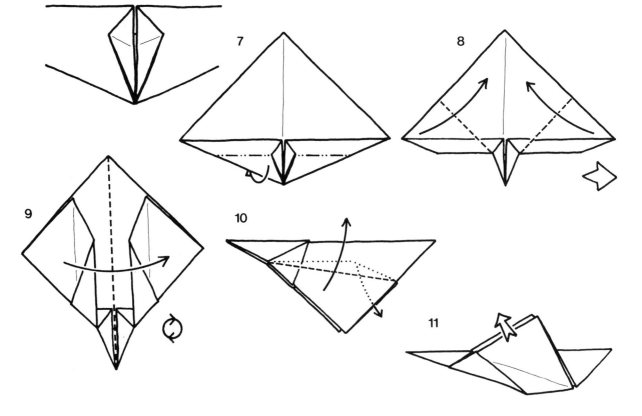

7

8

9

10

11

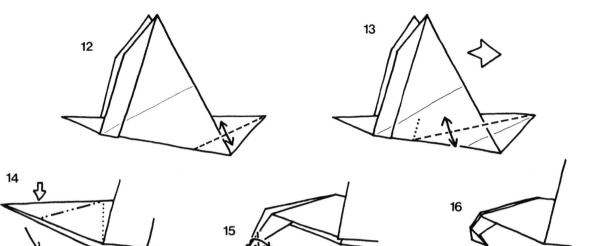

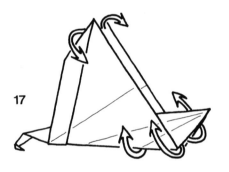

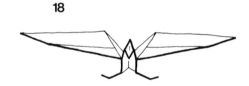

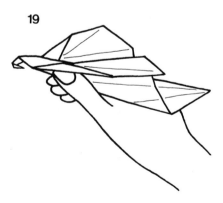

12. Fold the rear edge of the tail to the upper edge. Unfold. Repeat behind.

13. Fold the tail up from the bottom edge at the thick layer (X-ray line) to the rear corner. Unfold. Repeat behind.

14. Enlarged view of the head. Inside reverse fold the head down.

15. Outside reverse fold the beak.

16. Result.

17. Lower the wings and raise the tail flaps.

18. Front view.

19. Launch with gentle throw. The eagle should have a delicate, graceful flight. Adjust the elevation and angles of the tail flaps and wings for best performance.

18. Manta Ray

Designed by Michael LaFosse.

Use a square of paper. Twenty-pound bond works well.
Start with step 3 of the Soaring Eagle, 17.
1. Mountain fold the top of the squashed flap behind,
   wrapping it around the edges below it.
2. Step 1 in progress.
3. Mountain fold the bottom section behind along the
   horizontal diagonal crease.
4. Fold the lower edges to the vertical center line.

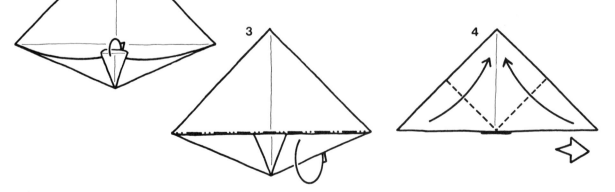

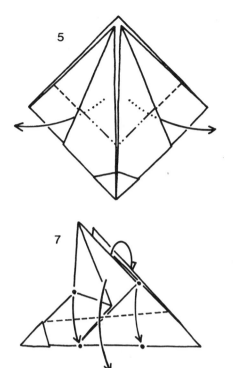

5

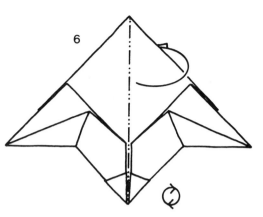

6

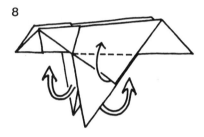

7

8

9

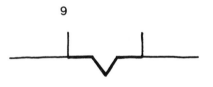

10

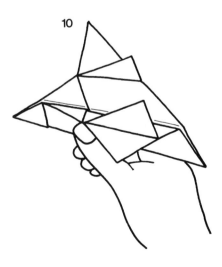

5. (The drawing is larger.) Inside reverse fold the wings as far as possible while still keeping the outer edges on each side even. (The near layer of each reverse fold is only half the width of the layer below it.)

6. Fold the model in half vertically by mountain folding the right side behind. Rotate the model clockwise.

7. Fold the wing down on each side, lining up the base of the flap on the upper surface with the bottom edge of the keel. (It may help to fold the flaps first as in step 8.)

8. Fold up the flap. Repeat behind. Raise the wings to a level position and lift the flaps straight up.

9. Front view.

10. Launch with a moderate throw.

19. Manta Jet

Designed by Michael LaFosse.

Use a square of paper. Start with step 8 of the Manta Ray, 18.

1. Inside reverse fold up the thick layer from inside the model (X-ray lines), pulling it up so that its forward edge is perpendicular to the top edges of the model.
2. Fold this tab over, tucking it down as far as it will go. Raise the wings.

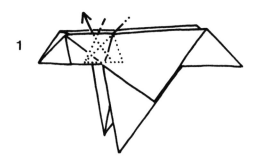

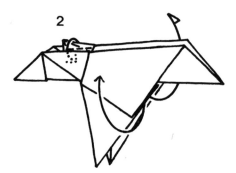

3. Inside reverse fold the keel up from the thick layer at the front to the base of each wing at the rear edge. Fold and unfold the tip of the wing to the point shown. Repeat behind. Lower the wings and raise the flaps straight up.
4. Front view. Adjust wing angles as in the drawing.
5. Launch with a moderate throw. Pressing down on the tail to open it slightly sometimes helps performance. This model flies very well when properly adjusted.

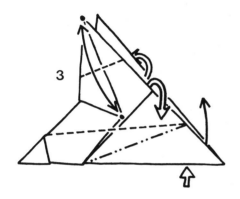

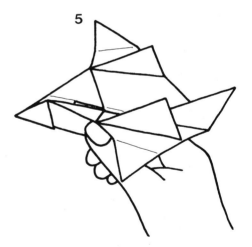

20. Flying Fish

Designed by Stephen Weiss.

1

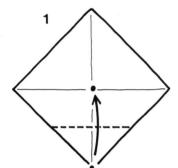

Use a square of paper.
1. Fold the bottom corner to the center of the square.
2. Fold the bottom edge to the horizontal center line. Unfold.
3. Fold the bottom edge to the crease made in step 2.
4. Fold the bottom up once more along the folded edge and existing crease.
5. Fold the bottom edges up to the vertical center line.
6. (The drawing is larger.) Turn the model over.

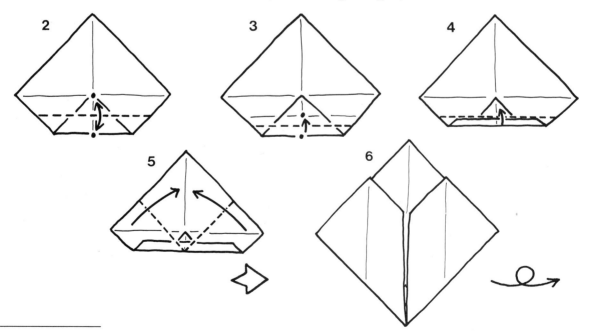

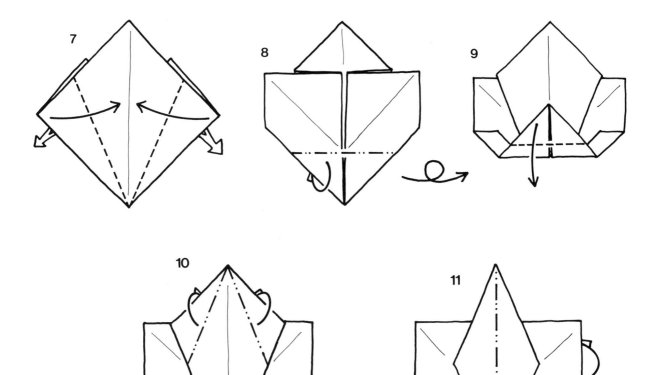

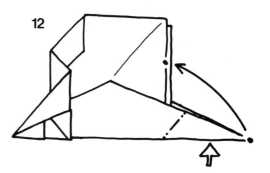

7. Fold the lower edges to the center line, allowing the paper behind to swing out.

8. Mountain fold the bottom corner behind where the diagonal creases intersect at the center line. Turn the model over.

9. Fold the corner back down so that the tip of the layer behind touches the fold (see step 10).

10. Mountain fold the upper edges of the center flap behind to the center line.

11. Fold the model in half vertically by mountain folding the right side behind. Rotate the model clockwise.

12. Inside reverse fold the tail up so that the reversed edge lies along the rear edges of the wings.

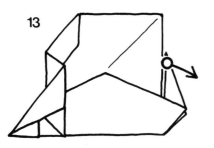

13

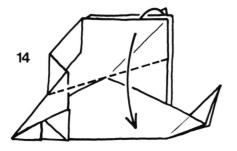

14

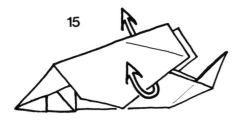

15

16

13. Pull the tail down so that the top edge lines up with the creases made in step 12. Pinch the lower edges to fix the new position (see step 14).

14. Fold the wing down on each side from the bottom of its vertical front edge across the highest point of the body.

15. Raise the wings.

16. Front view.

17. Hold as shown and launch with a moderate throw. Be sure the leading edges of the wings are flat and even and the tail is straight. Try launching the Flying Fish outside, throwing upward into a light breeze. To make the Flying Fish do a loop, pull the front of the wings away from each other to spread out the head area. Hold the model by one wing near the leading edge in a vertical position with the head pointing up. The belly should be towards you and the tail away from you. Throw the model straight up and it will loop away and back.

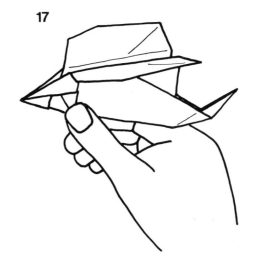

17

21. Swooping Hawk

Designed by Stephen Weiss.

Use an 8½ × 11″ sheet of paper.
1. Fold the lower left corner to the upper right corner. Rotate the model counterclockwise.
2. Fold up the bottom across the widest points.
3. Fold the model in half vertically. Unfold. Turn the model over.
4. Fold the bottom edges to the vertical center line.
5. (The drawing is larger.) Turn the model over.

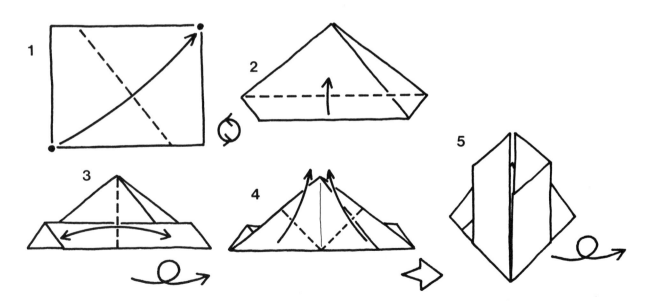

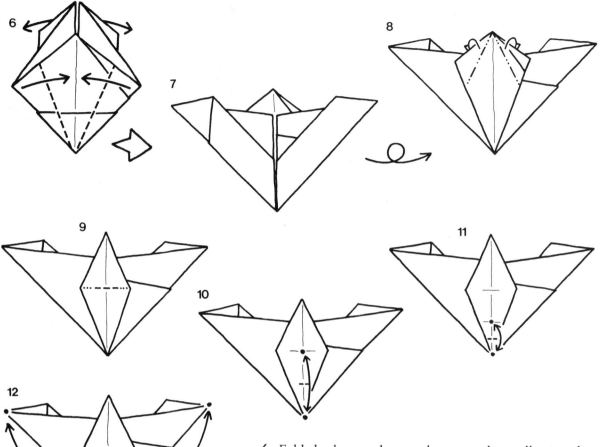

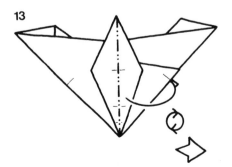

6. Fold the lower edges to the center line, allowing the paper behind to swing out.

7. (The drawing is larger.) Turn the model over.

8. Mountain fold the upper edges of the center flap behind to the center line.

9. Make a pinch mark between the widest points of the center flap.

10. Bring the bottom point of the model to the mark just made and pinch to mark the halfway point.

11. Bring the bottom point to the halfway mark and pinch again to determine the quarter mark.

12. Bring the tips of the wings down to the bottom point and pinch the edges to mark the halfway point.

13. Fold the model in half vertically by mountain folding the right side behind. Rotate the model clockwise.

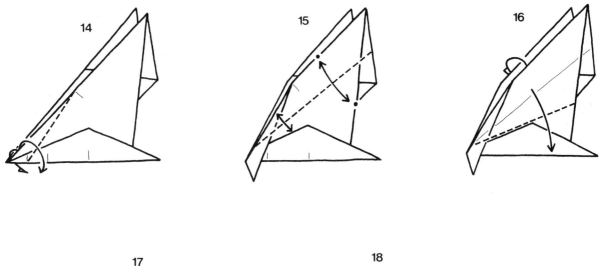

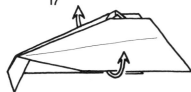

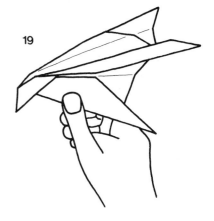

14. (The drawing is larger.) Outside reverse fold the head down from the quarter mark on the bottom edge of the model to the halfway point on the leading edge of each wing.

15. Fold the front of the leading edge of the wing to lie along the front upper edge of the body. The rear of the leading edge should touch the point of intersection indicated on the rear edges. Unfold. Repeat behind.

16. Fold the wing down on each side along the front upper edge of the body. The rear of the leading edge will line up with the bottom edge of the model.

17. Raise the wings.

18. Rear view.

19. Launch as shown with a gentle to hard throw. Adjust wing elevation and angles for best performance. The Swooping Hawk can also be launched like a flying wing. Spread out and flatten it somewhat, hold at the rear by the tail, and launch with a gentle push.

22. Flying Nun

Designed by Stephen Weiss.

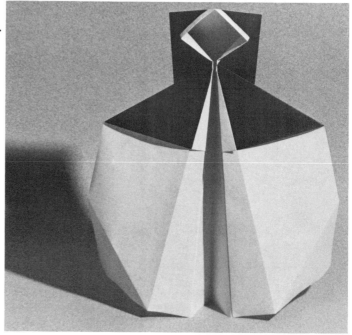

Use a square of paper, black or blue on one side, white on the other.

1. With the white side up, mountain fold the top edge behind, folding over a very narrow strip.
2. Fold the top edges to the vertical center line.
3. Turn the model over.

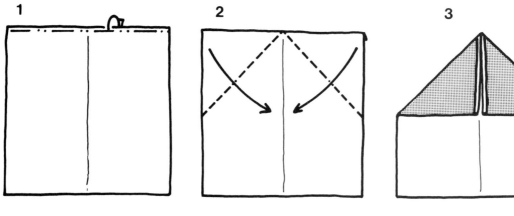

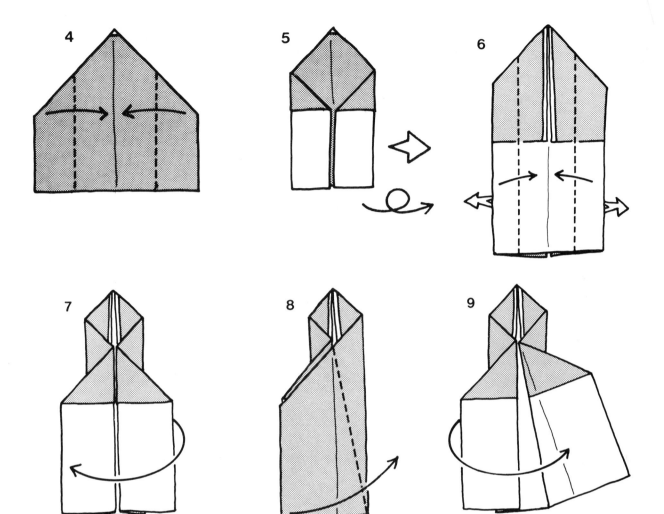

4. Fold the left and right vertical edges to the center line.
5. Turn the model over.
6. (The drawing is larger.) Fold the left and right vertical edges to the center line, allowing the paper behind to swing out.
7. Fold the right near surface to the left.
8. Fold it back again from the bottom right corner to its upper edge at the center of the model.
9. Fold the left near surface to the right.

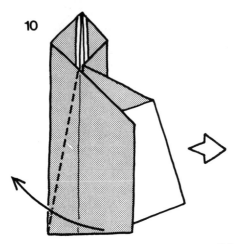

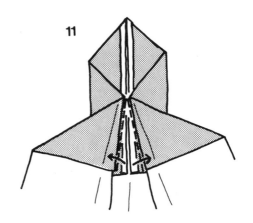

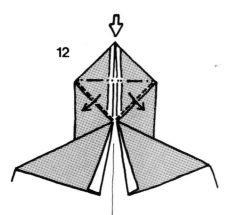

10. Fold it back again from the bottom left corner to its upper edge at the center of the model.
11. Enlarged view of the top of the model. Fold the flap on each side of the chest to the outside, wrapping it around the folded edge.
12. Press down the top of the head to open the face and squash down as shown.
13. Make the mountain and valley folds on the center section and pinch up a "tail fin" as shown in final drawings.
14. Mountain fold the lower corners behind so that the bottom edges lie along the creases shown on the habit.

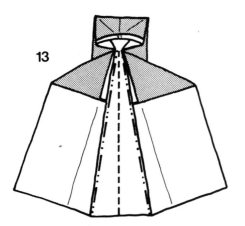

15. Open the face so it is a square diamond shape. Unfold the corner flaps.

16. Side view.

17. Front view. Note that the back of the head is rounded and convex.

18. Hold as shown and launch with a gentle push. The nun should float smoothly. The corner flaps tend to rise too much after creasing, so flatten them so they are only slightly elevated. The degree to which the face is open and the levelness of the shoulders also affect flight. You may want to reinforce the creases of the tail fin.

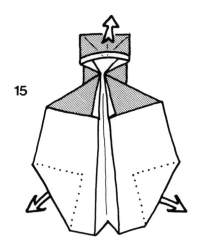

15

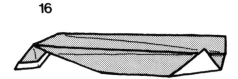

16

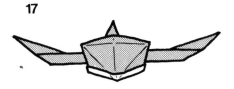

17

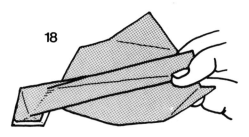

18

23. Flying Bat II

Designed by Max Hulme.

Use a square of thin paper, black or brown. Start with step 5 of the Flying Bird, 16.

1. Fold the bottom edges of the near flaps to the center line.
2. Pleat each doubled flap in thirds starting at the bottom.
3. Unfold.
4. Pleat each doubled flap in thirds starting at the top.

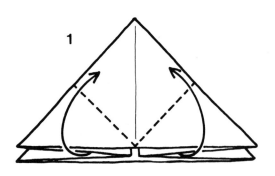

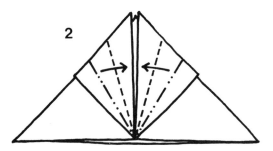

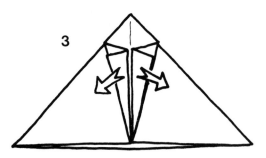

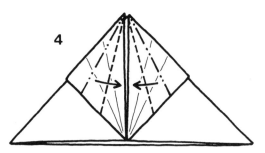

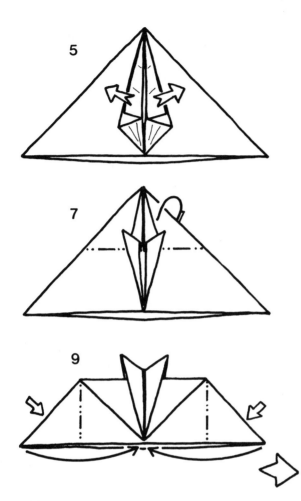
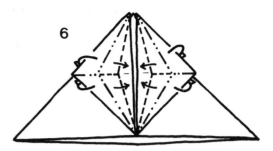
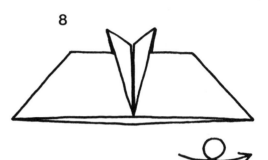
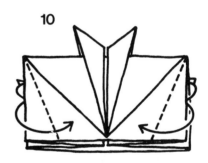

5. Unfold.
6. Pleat along the top and bottom creases at the same time as far as the horizontal center line. Pinch up the excess paper at the center, putting in the short valley and mountain folds.
7. Mountain fold the top behind to the bottom edge.
8. Turn the model over.
9. Inside reverse fold the outer corners to the center of the bottom edge.
10. (The drawing is larger.) Fold the vertical edge of the near flap on each side to lie along the lower edge of the triangular section. Mountain fold the far edges behind to match.

11

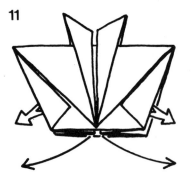

12

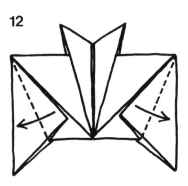

13

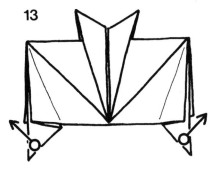

14

15

16

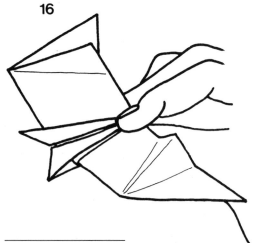

11. Pull out the paper between the near and far flaps on each side.
12. Fold the edge lying along the triangular section to the vertical edge on each side. Repeat behind.
13. Pull the wing corners out and adjust the open area on each wing so that it appears square when viewed from the rear.
14. Mountain fold along the center line to raise the wings. This is the bottom of the bat (shown in the photo). Turn the model over.
15. Front view.
16. Hold as shown and launch gently. The bat should glide smoothly. Adjust wing elevation for best flight. Bending the ears down or up slightly may help.

24. Penta-Flinger

Designed by Ed Sullivan.

You will need five equal rectangles of 2 × 3 proportion. 5 × 7½″ is a good size. They should be made of light card stock for best results.

Fold each rectangle as shown in steps 1–10. Be sure each unit is folded the same way.

1. Fold the top and bottom edges to the center line but leave a small space in the middle.
2. Starting from the lower left corner, fold the upper left corner to the center line. Unfold. Starting from the upper right corner, fold the lower right corner to the center line. Unfold.

1

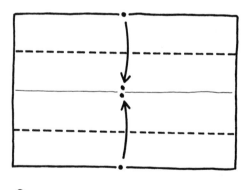

2

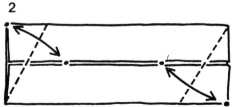

3

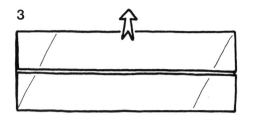

4

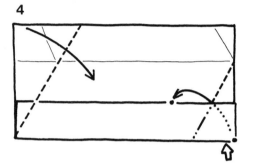

3. Unfold the top half of the rectangle.
4. Fold the left side in along the diagonal crease, extending it to the upper edge. Inside reverse fold the lower right corner along the diagonal creases.
5. Fold the top edge back down to the center along the existing crease.
6. Fold the left end in, leaving a small gap at the upper left corner. The crease should be perpendicular to the bottom edge.
7. First make separately the valley and mountain creases on the left end. Then fold the unit in half, bottom to top, and at the same time fold the left end in, pushing in the area at the bottom.
8. Mountain fold the lower left corner around the edge behind. Unfold.
9. Open out.
10. Rotate the unit clockwise.

5

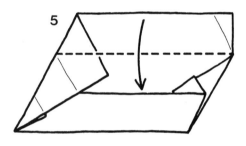

6

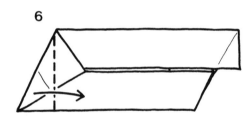

7

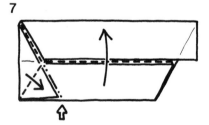

8

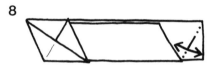

9

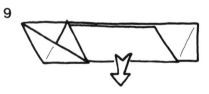

10

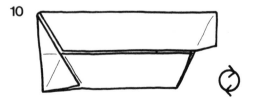

11. Fit two units together as shown. The doubled end of one unit fits into the pocket end of the other unit.
12. Mountain fold the end flap around the edge behind, tucking it into the pocket. This locks the units together.
13. Join a third unit in the same manner.
14. Complete by adding the two remaining units. As the last connection to close the ring is made, the Penta-Flinger will become three-dimensional, with a ridge along the center line of the rim. It sometimes helps to reinforce this crease by squeezing, especially at the corner joints.

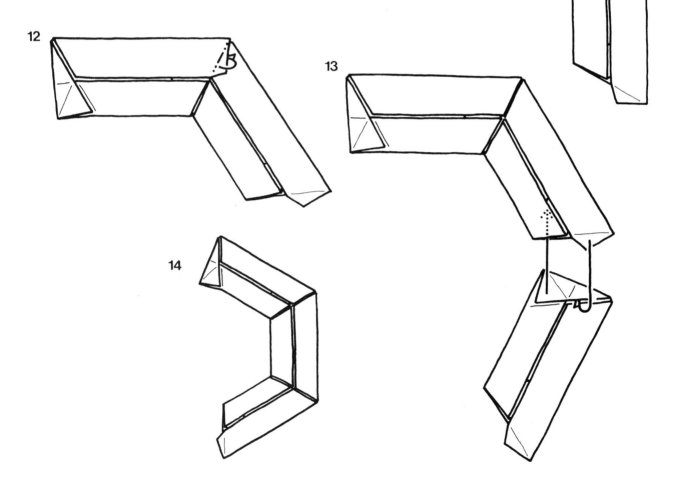

15. Complete. Turn the model over.
16. Top view.
17. Hold as shown and throw with a flick of the wrist as one would throw a flying disk.

15

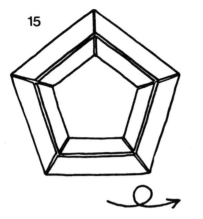

16

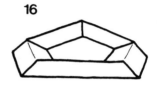

17

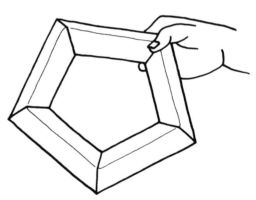

25. Arc Wing

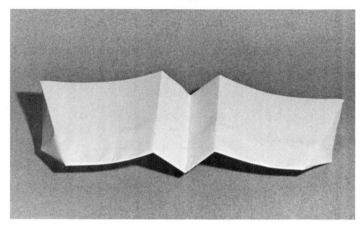

Designed by Stephen Weiss.
Based on a rectangular wing design by
    Hans R. Bergan.

Use a square of paper.

1. Fold the bottom edge to the horizontal center line.
2. Fold the outer edges of the bottom corners to the upper edge of the doubled paper.
3. Fold the bottom edge to the upper edge of the doubled paper, including turned-in corners, and then fold the whole section over two times.
4. (The drawing is larger.) Inside reverse fold the lower corners. The mountain folds will wrap around the edges behind.

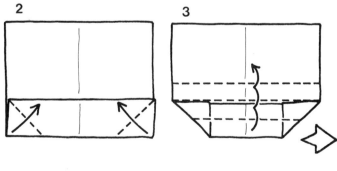

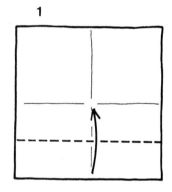

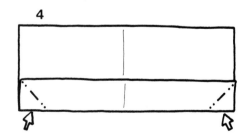

5

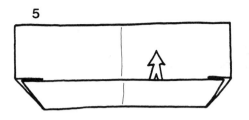

6

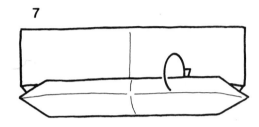

7

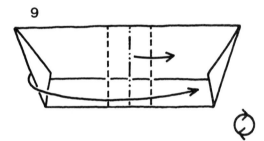

8

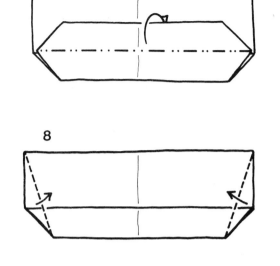

9

10

11

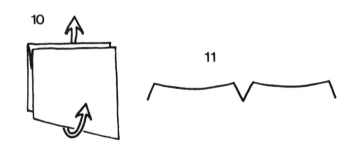

12

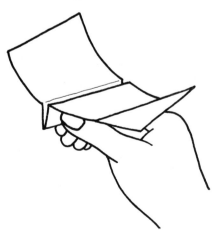

5. Pull out the inner layer.
6. Fold the layer behind again, wrapping it around the inside reversed corner on each side. This locks the outer edges together.
7. Step 6 in progress.
8. Fold the sides in from the lower to upper corners on each side.
9. Pleat the body as shown. Each half of the pleat is $1/8$ of the length of the bottom edge. Rotate the model clockwise.
10. Raise the wings. Unfold the flaps down.
11. Front view. Curve the wings upward in a shallow arc.
12. Launch with a gentle throw.

26. Art Deco Wing

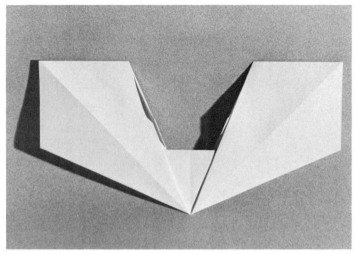

Designed by Michael LaFosse.

Use a square of paper. Crease one diagonal and fold the square in half along the other diagonal.
1. Fold the bottom edges to the vertical center line.
2. Squash down each flap symmetrically, matching up the center lines on the underside.

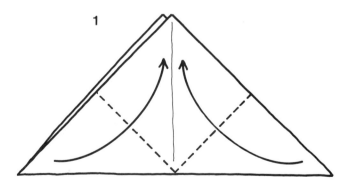

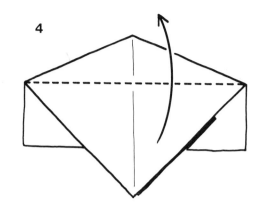

3

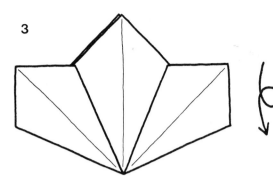

4

5

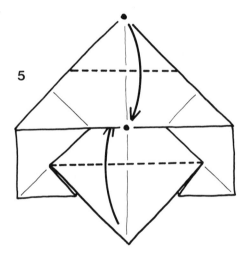

6

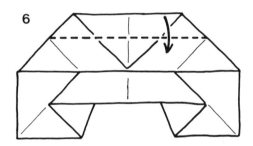

7

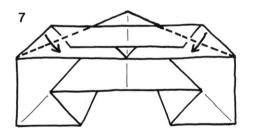

3. Result. Turn the model over top to bottom.
4. Fold the near layer up as far as possible.
5. Fold the top down to the center of the folded edge. Fold the bottom up as far as possible, tucking it under the folded edge.
6. Fold the top down from where the crease lines meet the left and right upper edges.
7. Fold the left and right upper edges down to the folded edge.

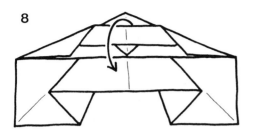

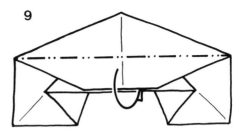

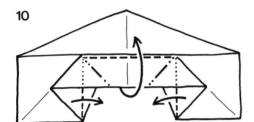

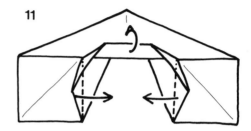

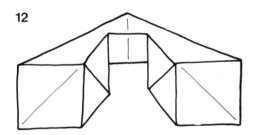

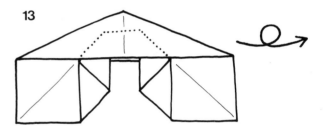

8. Swing the flap down.
9. Mountain fold the flap inside the model. This is easiest to do if the model is partly unfolded, or opened out.
10. Pull up the lower edge at the center, folding it over the edge above. Push in the sides at the same time.
11. Step 10 in progress.
12. Complete. Tuck the overlapping flap inside the top of the model.
13. X-ray lines show position of the flap inside. Turn the model over.

14

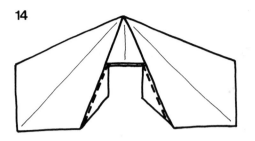

14. Fold the flaps straight up.
15. Front view.
16. Hold as shown and launch with a slight forward push.

15

16

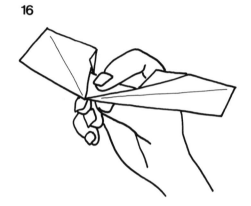

27. Monoplane

Designed by Stephen Weiss.

Use a square of paper.
1. Fold the bottom corner to the center of the square.
2. Fold the top half down along the diagonal.
3. Fold the top edges to the vertical center line.
4. (The drawing is larger.) Fold the edges at the center to the upper edges.

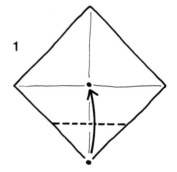

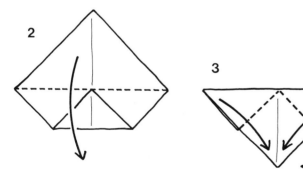

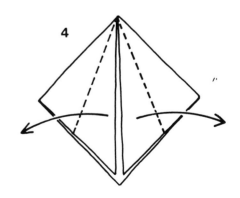

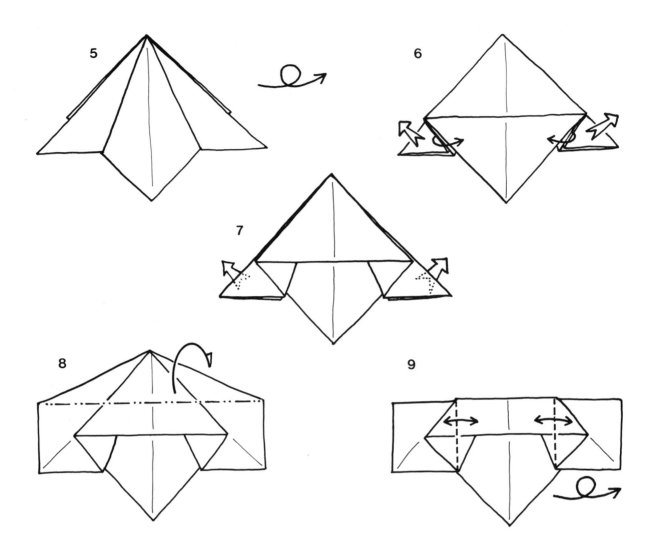

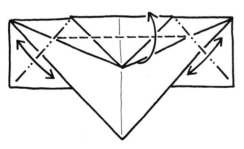

5. Turn the model over.
6. Pull out the near layer on each side and re-place it in front.
7. Unfold the flaps up from behind.
8. Mountain fold the top of the model behind.
9. Fold the triangular flap in on each side. Unfold. Turn the model over.
10. Mountain fold the upper corners behind. Unfold. Fold up the thick layer between the diagonal mountain creases.

11

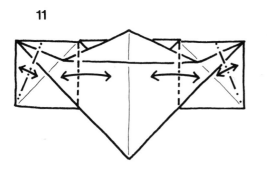

12

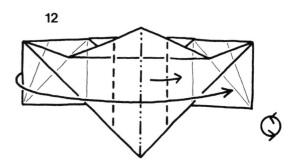

13

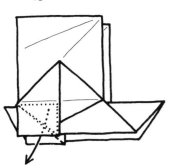

14

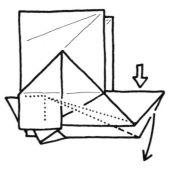

15

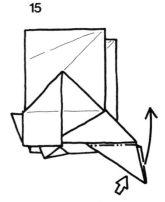

16

11. Mountain fold the outer edges behind to the diagonal creases. Unfold. Fold each wing in at its base. Unfold.

12. Pleat the body by making the mountain and valley folds shown. Rotate the model counterclockwise.

13. Inside reverse fold the thick layer inside the front of the body down as far as possible (X-ray lines).

14. Inside reverse fold the top edge of the body down from the thick layer at the front to the lower rear corners.

15. Inside reverse fold the tail up so that all the bottom edges are even.

16. Lower the wings and fold the "wheel" flaps straight down.

17. Front view.

18. Hold the Monoplane by the tab under the nose and throw gently. Be sure the leading edges are well creased and flat, and wing angles are symmetrical. The center diagonal crease on each wing should be flattened out almost completely. Sometimes spreading the tail end apart slightly improves stability.

17

18

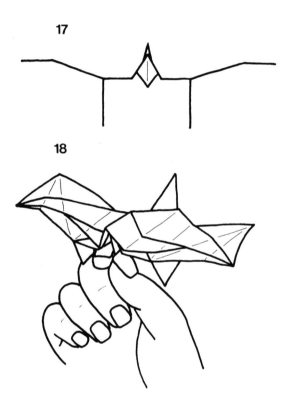

28. Gliding Swan

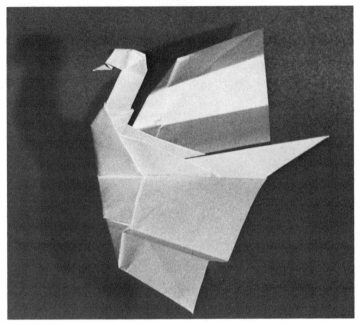

Designed by Stephen Weiss.

Use a square of white paper. Start with step 13 of the Flapping Bird, 15.

1. Inside reverse fold the tail section up from the bottom of the wings so that the rear edges are even.
2. Turn the rear edges of the tail inside to the front edge of the tail.
3. Lower the wing and make the fold shown. The front will remain concave.

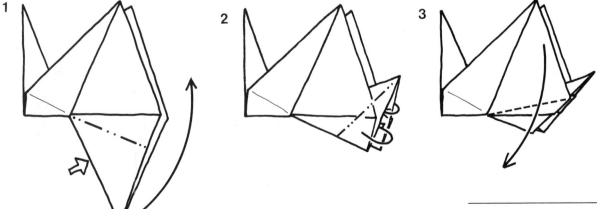

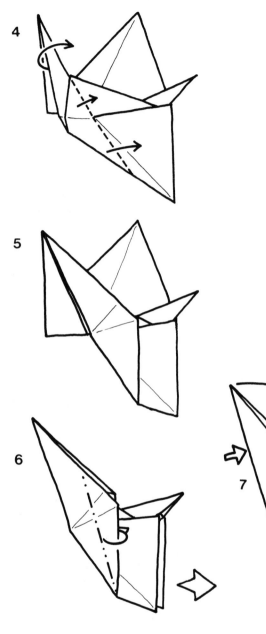

4. Fold the near side of the neck to the right and flatten the model.
5. Result. Be sure the outer layer of paper is tightly wrapped around the edge of the wing near the neck. Repeat steps 3 and 4 behind.
6. Narrow the neck flap by mountain folding the rear edge behind as far as possible to the front edge. Repeat behind.
7. (The drawing is larger.) Inside reverse fold the neck backwards, starting from the point of the chest. The thick layers inside must be reversed with it. Position the fold so that the reversed edge is perpendicular to the edges of the swan's back.
8. Narrow the neck starting from the thick layer (X-ray line) by mountain folding the front edges behind until the corner touches the rear edge of the neck. Repeat behind. Note that the fold does not extend to the top point.

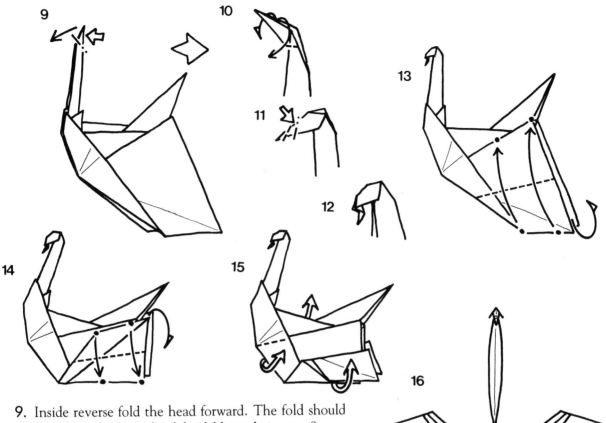

9. Inside reverse fold the head forward. The fold should pass through the ends of the folds made in step 8.

10. Enlarged view of the head. Outside reverse fold the head downward. The fold should pass through the intersection of the lower edge of the head and the front of the neck.

11. Form the bill by making two inside reverse folds. Make the right one and then the left one.

12. Result.

13. Fold up the lower edge of the wing on each side so that it lies along the base of the wing.

14. Fold the edge down on each side to the bottom edge.

15. Fold the wings up to crease the paper at the front. Then unfold them out into position.

16. Front view.

17. Hold underneath as shown and launch with a gentle to moderate throw. Adjust wing angles for best flight. This model doesn't look like it will fly, but it does.

29. Seagull

Designed by Yoshihide Momotani.

Use a square of paper.

1. Fold the square in half diagonally, right to left.
2. Fold 1/3 of the near layer to the right.
3. Fold the model in half by mountain folding the top behind to the bottom.
4. (The drawing is larger.) Pull the top edge down between the edges of the triangular layer. This is called an "outside crimp." It is easier if the mountain folds are made separately first.

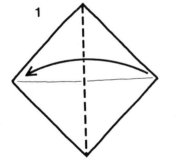

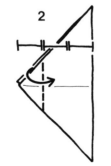

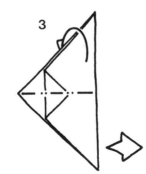

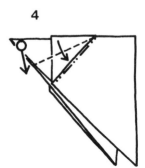

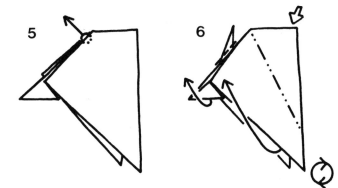

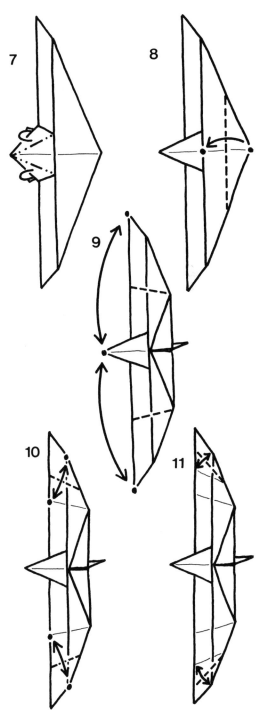

5. Pull out the pleated triangular flap. Swing it forward to a position where it will just touch the folded edge you will make in step 8.

6. Raise the wing and tail while pressing in the upper corner. Flatten this corner down symmetrically. Rotate the model clockwise.

7. Mountain fold the rear edges of the tail behind to the center line.

8. Fold the front tip to the center of the edge formed by the flattened corner.

9. The edge of the head should touch the front edge. If it is too far back or too far forward, adjust the amount it was raised in step 5. Fold the tip of the wings to the tip of the tail. Unfold.

10. Fold the corner which is closest to the tip on the front edge of each wing so that it touches the rear edge of the wing at the crease. Unfold.

11. On each side fold the outer front edge adjacent to the crease made in step 10 so that it lies along that crease. Unfold.

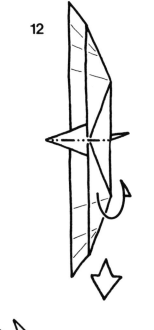

12

12. Fold the model in half by mountain folding the bottom to the top behind.
13. (The drawing is larger.) Inside reverse fold the head down, starting even with the leading edges of the raised wings.
14. Fold the wings down along the front upper edges of the body (hidden by layers). Then raise the wings.
15. Front view.
16. Hold the Seagull as shown and launch with a gentle to moderate throw. The most critical factor affecting flight is how much the very last wing section on each side is turned down. The Seagull tends to flap its wings in flight, especially if made from large or thin paper, or thrown hard. For a more gliding flight, bend the last wing sections farther down. Try launching from a second story in a light breeze.

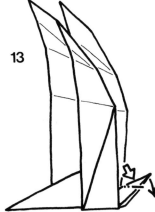

13

14

15

16

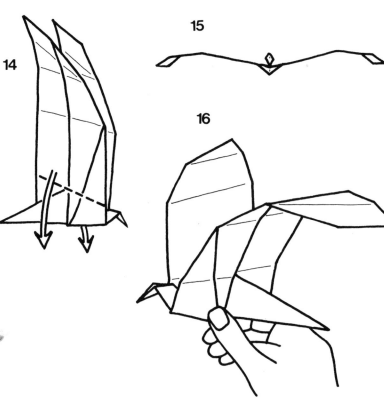

30. Mach III Jet

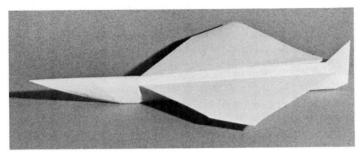

Designed by Yoshihide Momotani.

Use a square of paper.

1. Fold the left edges to the center line.
2. Mountain fold the left tip behind to the point on the center line between the turned-in corners.
3. (The drawing is larger.) Fold the left front edges to the center line. Turn the model over, top to bottom.
4. Swing the flap to the left. At the same time open out the paper on the bottom half and flatten it forward.
5. Result. Turn the model over, top to bottom.
6. Fold the top to the bottom and tuck the extended side of the flap inside the pocket on the lower half.

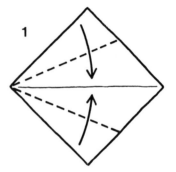

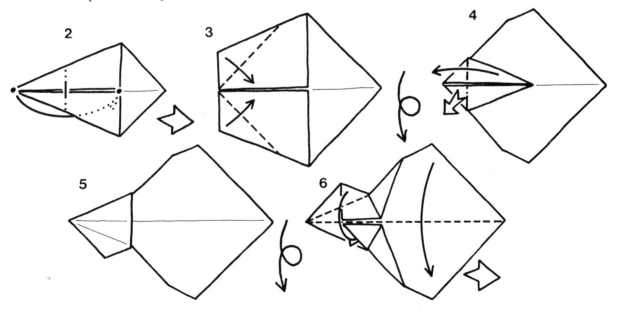

7

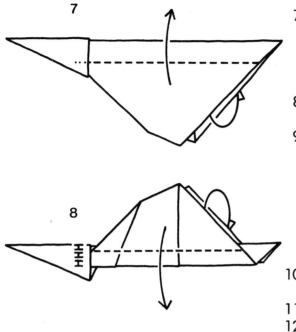

8

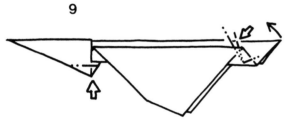

9

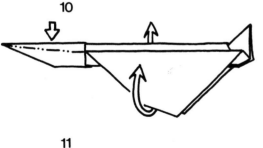

10

11

7. (The drawing is larger.) Fold the wing up on each side so that the fold is parallel to the top edge of the model. The wing will slide up under the layer at the front and should protrude from it ⅔ of the way from the bottom edge of the body to the top edge. (See step 8.)

8. Fold the wing down on each side starting ⅓ of the way from the top edge to the bottom edge.

9. Inside reverse fold the bottom of the nose into the body. Raise the tail by making the small crimp at the rear. First, partially inside reverse fold the tail down to make the mountain folds. Then raise the tail to make the valley folds, pressing down the paper in front of them. This is called an "inside crimp." The paper at the lower rear corners will swivel up (small mountain fold).

10. Raise the wings to a level position. Press down the top of the nose to 3-D it slightly.

11. Front view.

12. Hold as shown by just one or both sides of the body, and launch with a moderate throw.

12

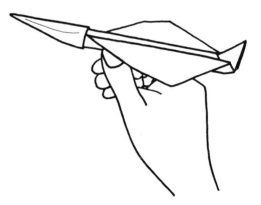

31. Delta Jet (and Stand)

Designed by Marvin Goody.

DELTA JET

Use a square of paper.

1. Bring the lower edge of one side to the vertical center line but do not crease.
2. Press the corner down as shown. Fold the top down over it, and pinch to mark the point on the center line. Return the sheet to its flat position.

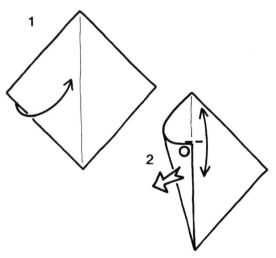

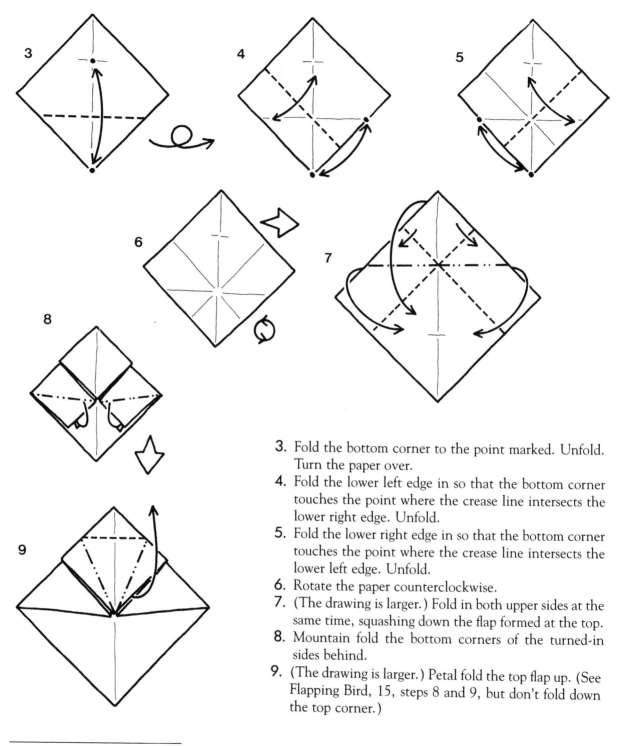

3. Fold the bottom corner to the point marked. Unfold. Turn the paper over.
4. Fold the lower left edge in so that the bottom corner touches the point where the crease line intersects the lower right edge. Unfold.
5. Fold the lower right edge in so that the bottom corner touches the point where the crease line intersects the lower left edge. Unfold.
6. Rotate the paper counterclockwise.
7. (The drawing is larger.) Fold in both upper sides at the same time, squashing down the flap formed at the top.
8. Mountain fold the bottom corners of the turned-in sides behind.
9. (The drawing is larger.) Petal fold the top flap up. (See Flapping Bird, 15, steps 8 and 9, but don't fold down the top corner.)

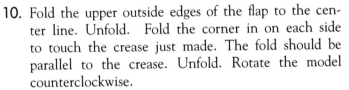

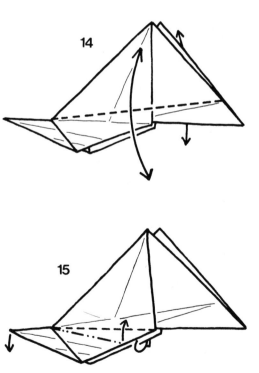

10. Fold the upper outside edges of the flap to the center line. Unfold. Fold the corner in on each side to touch the crease just made. The fold should be parallel to the crease. Unfold. Rotate the model counterclockwise.

11. Mountain fold the inner edges of the front layers behind to the front edges. Unfold.

12. Mountain fold the bottom behind to the top and fold the top half of the front flap down.

13. Fold the bottom up to precrease the tail from halfway between the folded edge and the center crease of the front layer to ¼ of the way up the rear edges. Unfold.

14. Fold down the wing on each side from the nose to where the crease touches the rear edge. Unfold.

15. Outside crimp the paper below the wing on each side so that the mountain fold lies along the wing crease made in step 14. The nose will tilt down as these crimps are put in together.

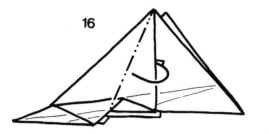

16

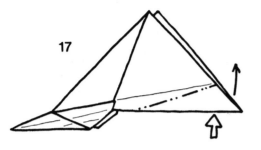

17

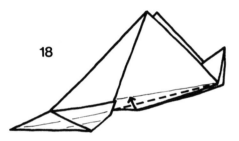

18

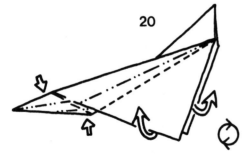

20

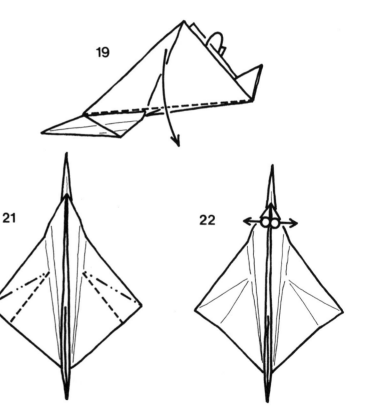

16. Mountain fold the rear edge of the near layer behind to the front edge along the pre-crease. This will lock in the crimp. Repeat behind on the other side.
17. Inside reverse fold the tail up along the pre-creases.
18. Fold up all the bottom layers so that the long edges lie along the base of the wing. This is a very narrow fold.
19. Fold down the wings.
20. Make the mountain and valley folds on the wings to form the body. Press the top and bottom of the nose to shape it. Rotate the model clockwise.
21. Top view. Put in the wing-shaping creases. The mountain creases lie along the layers below and the valley creases are parallel to the leading edges. They can be made by crimping the wings so that the rear edges are even, and then unfolding.
22. Gently pull the paper on each side of the "cabin" to round the front.

23. Result.
24. Front view.
25. Hold the Delta Jet by the nose and launch gently. It should float smoothly.

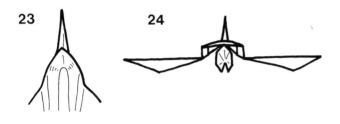

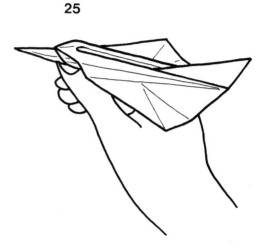

STAND

Use a square of paper the same size as that used for the Delta Jet.

1. Fold the upper edges to the center line.
2. Rabbit ear the bottom triangle (see Soaring Eagle, 17, step 1), so that the top and bottom edges of the finished rabbit ear evenly straddle the lower edges of the turned-in sides.
3. Squash the flap symmetrically.

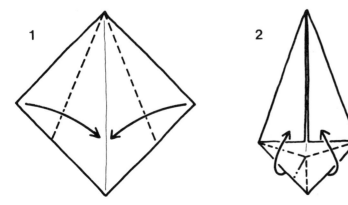

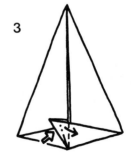

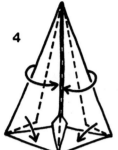

4. Fold the upper sides to the center line to crease. Fold the edges of each bottom corner together to crease. Squeeze the vertical center valley crease to obtain the bottom view in step 7.

5. Inside reverse fold the tip at an oblique upward angle.

6. Result. Turn the stand around.

7. Bottom view.

8. Insert the tip of the stand into the pocket under the cabin of the Delta Jet. If used as a decoration, try the jet in silver foil paper and the stand in black. The wing-shaping creases can be eliminated for this purpose.

32. Maple Seed

Designed by Stephen Weiss.
Inspired by a maple seed from a strip of
paper by Michael LaFosse.

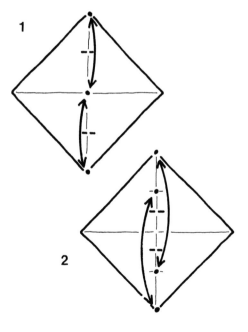

Use a square of thin paper. A 3 to 4″ square of airmail paper
or a 6″ square of origami paper works well.

1. Make both diagonal valley creases. Then bring the top
   and bottom corners to the center and pinch to mark
   points on the vertical center line. Return the corners.

2. Bring the top corner to touch the mark made on the
   bottom half in step 1 and make a pinch mark. Return
   the corner. Bring the bottom corner to the mark made
   on the top half in step 1 and make a pinch mark.
   Return the corner.

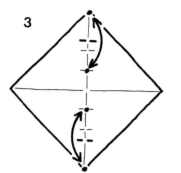

3

3. Bring the top corner to the mark made on the top half in step 2 and make a pinch mark. Return the corner. Bring the bottom corner to the mark made on the bottom half in step 2 and make a pinch mark. Return the corner.

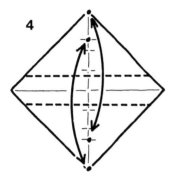

4

4. Bring the top corner to the last mark made on the bottom half and crease all the way across. Unfold. Bring the bottom corner to the last mark made on the top half and crease all the way across. Unfold.

5. Result. Rotate the paper clockwise.

6. Fold the upper edge on each side in to lie along the vertical crease on each side of the center line.

7. Fold the right side in along the right vertical crease.

5

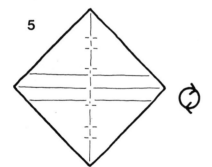

6

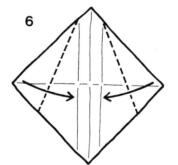

7

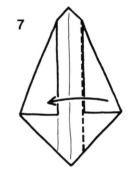

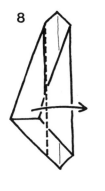

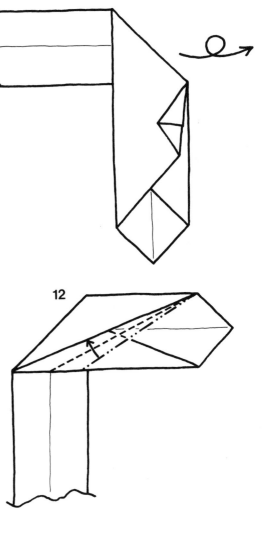

8. Fold the left side over the right along the left vertical crease.
9. Fold in the protruding corner so that it is even with the right vertical edge at the top but angled slightly in at the bottom.
10. Mountain fold the top behind to the left, starting at the top of the turned-in corner, so that it is perpendicular to the lower section.
11. (The drawing is larger.) Result. Turn the model over.
12. Crimp the blade so that the valley fold touches the vertical center line. The mountain fold will lie along the edge of the upper layer.

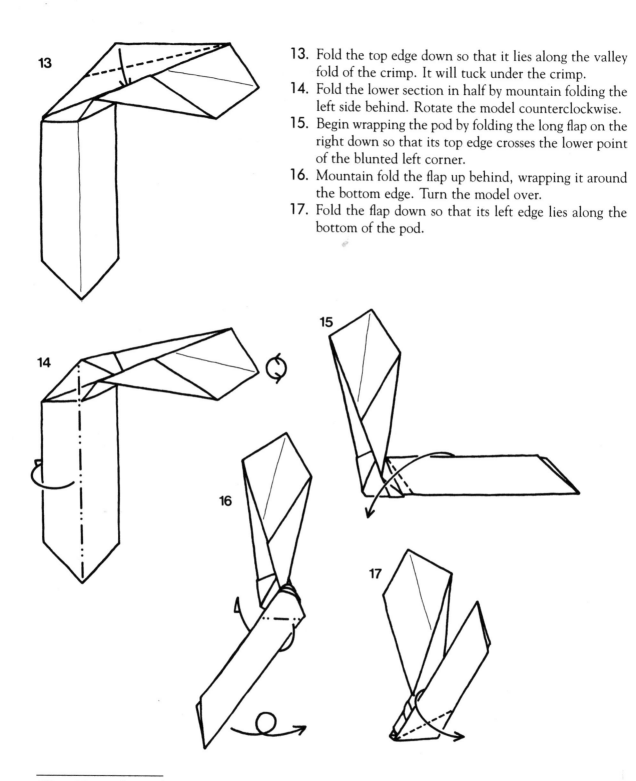

13. Fold the top edge down so that it lies along the valley fold of the crimp. It will tuck under the crimp.

14. Fold the lower section in half by mountain folding the left side behind. Rotate the model counterclockwise.

15. Begin wrapping the pod by folding the long flap on the right down so that its top edge crosses the lower point of the blunted left corner.

16. Mountain fold the flap up behind, wrapping it around the bottom edge. Turn the model over.

17. Fold the flap down so that its left edge lies along the bottom of the pod.

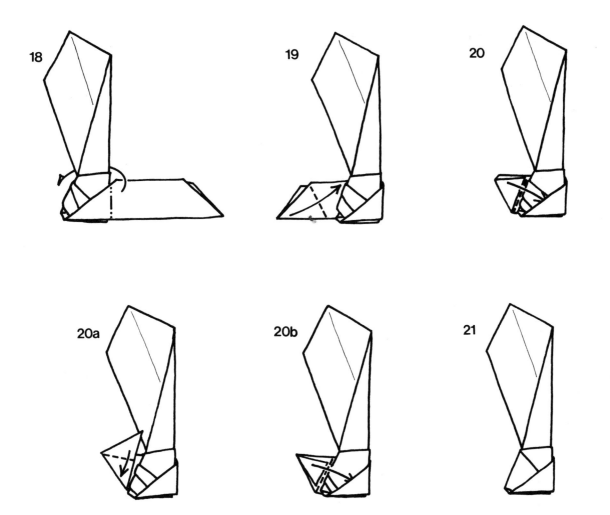

18. Mountain fold the flap behind, wrapping it around the right side of the pod.
19. Fold up the tip of the flap.
20. Fold the end of the flap down over the left edge of the pod and tuck it into the pocket.
20. a. If very thin paper or a larger square is used there may be more excess paper at the end of the flap. If so, simply fold it over once more.
20. b. Then tuck it into the pocket.
21. Result.

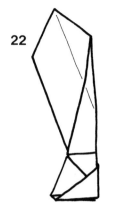

22. The Maple Seed can be made to spin flatter by extending the center crease of the blade through the leading edge near the pod and bending the front down very slightly.

23. Hold the Maple Seed at the pod with the blade down and throw it straight up into the air. It should "helicopter" down. The smooth convex side should be uppermost as it spins down for best results. Try dropping it from a height.

24. The flight of the Maple Seed.

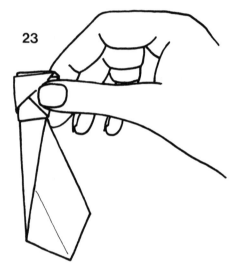

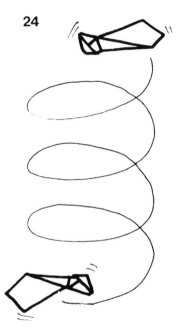

Bibliography

This list contains only books (or articles) which use origami for making things that fly, or which relate to flying origami in some way. Although some of the books are in Japanese, the diagrams can still be understood by anyone familiar with standard origami notation.

Barnaby, Ralph S. *How to Make and Fly Paper Airplanes.* New York: Four Winds Press (a division of Scholastic Magazines, Inc.), 1968.
A definitive guide to aeronautics as applied to paper airplanes. Little true origami, but educational.

Bergan, Hans R. *The Lingore Paper Airplane Folding Manual.* Potsdam, New York: Lingore Press, 1981; distributed by Charles E. Tuttle Company, Rutland, Vermont.
Origami combined with paper cutting and stapling is used to create many varieties of flying wings and both one- and two-piece airplanes.

Botermans, Jack. *Paper Flight.* Devon, England: David & Charles, 1984. Unreviewed.

Campbell, Morris. *Advanced Paper Aircraft Construction.* Sydney: Cornstalk Publishing (a division of Angus and Robertson Publishers); London: Angus and Robertson (UK) Ltd., 1983.
This appealing little book contains fourteen origami models of airplanes, darts, and wings. Only three models are cut. The paper proportions used are $1:\sqrt{2}$ and other standard international proportions and sizes.

Grater, Michael. *Cut & Fold Paper Spaceships that Fly.* New York: Dover Publications, Inc., 1981.
Contains cut-out pages for sixteen colorful airplanes made by cutting, folding, weighting with paper clips, and taping.

Kasahara, Kunihiko. *Origami Made Easy.* Tokyo: Japan Publications, Inc., 1973.
This attractive general origami book for beginners includes five airplanes and a flying eagle.

Lewis, Shari; Oppenheimer, Lillian. *Folding Paper Toys.* Briarcliff Manor, NY: A Scarborough Book, Stein and Day, 1963.
This charming little book contains boats, flying objects, dollhouse furniture, tricks, puppets, and party favors. Some models involve cutting.

Mander, Jerry; Dipple, George; Gossage, Howard. *The Great International Paper Airplane Book.* New York: Simon and Schuster, 1967.

This well-known book presents winners of the Scientific American First International Paper Airplane Competition. Most entries use origami in whole or in part.

Momotani, Yoshihide. *Sora Tobu Tori No Origami* (Origami Birds Flying in the Sky). Tokyo: Seinbundo Shinkō Sha, 1977.

This book by one of Japan's leading creators of origami contains four dozen flying origami birds of all kinds. Some involve cutting, but most do not. The birds are pictured in eight full-page color photos and numerous black-and-white photos. Japanese text.

Momotani. *Norimono Origami* (Origami Vehicles). Tokyo: Seinbundo Shinkō Sha, 1978.

One of the author's best books, it contains a section on origami airplanes, as well as trains, cars, and boats. Color and black-and-white photos. Japanese text.

Momotani. *Origami Tejina* (Origami Magic). Tokyo: Seinbundo Shinkō Sha, 1977.

A book of origami toys and action models, and simple objects, animals, and birds; it also contains a number of airplanes, flying birds, gliders, kites, and a flying dragonfly. Japanese text.

Most of Momotani's other books each contain at least a few origami airplanes and/or flying birds.

Morris, Scot. "Fancy Flights: The World's Most Mysterious Paper Airplane." *Omni,* April 1984.

Discusses the history, development, and aerodynamics of the Kline/Fogleman wing and gives directions and cut-out pages for making the Kline/Fogleman paper airplane.

Nakamura, Eiji. *Flying Origami: Origami from Pure Fun to True Science.* Tokyo: Japan Publications, Inc., 1972.

Twenty-eight original airplanes made from rectangles in the proportion $1:\sqrt{2}$, which the author calls the "True Rectangle." Some models involve cutting and taping.

Nakamura. *Kamiori Hikō-ki* (Origami Airplanes). Tokyo: Nihon Bungei Sha, 1977.

A further collection of thirty-seven uncut origami airplanes, most using paper in the proportion $1:\sqrt{2}$. Also contains three elaborate cutout airplanes. Japanese text.

The following books by Nakamura may contain some duplication of subject matter. They all have Japanese text.

Tanoshii Origami Hikō-ki Kessaku 30 Sen: Kagaku-Teki Origami e no Apurōchi (30 Selected Masterpieces of Enjoyable Origami Airplanes: An Approach toward Scientific Origami). (Shin-hokei Series, 2.) Tokyo: Nichibō Shuppan Sha, 1973.

Teihon Sora Tobu Origami Sōshu (Standard Edition of Collection of Flying Origami). Tokyo: Nichibō Shuppan Sha, 1976.

Yoku Tobu Hikō Origami Sen (Flying Origami Airplanes, Selected). Tokyo: Tokyo Shoten, 1975.

Yoku Tobu Origami Hikō-ki: Sugu Oreru Tojikomi Yōshi Tsuki (Flying Origami Airplanes: With Interleaves That are Easy to Fold). Fujisawa: Ikeda Shoten, 1975.

Yoku Tobu Orisen Tsuki Hikō Origami (Flying Origami Airplanes with Folding Lines). Tokyo: Tokyo Shoten, 1975.

Sora Tobu Origami Kessaku 30 Sen: Tanoshimi no Origami Kara Kagahu-Teki Origami e (Flying Origami: 30 Selected Masterpieces: From Origami Play to Scientific Origami). Tokyo: Nichibō, 1973.

Nakano, Dokuotei. *Origami Kun 1: Yasashii Origami* (Easy Origami). Tokyo: Takahashii Shoten.

Nakano. *Origami Kun 2: Tanoshii Origami* (Enjoyable Origami). Tokyo: Takahashii Shoten.

Nakano. *Origami Kun 3: Yukaina Origami* (Pleasant Origami). Tokyo: Takahashii Shoten.

These three books of general origami by Nakano each contain about seven or eight airplanes and gliders. Japanese text.

Simon, Seymour. *The Paper Airplane Book.* New York: Viking Press, 1971.
    Similar to the Barnaby book, but on an elementary school level. Experimental approach to aerodynamic theory and a few simple airplanes.

Slade, Richard. *Paper Aeroplanes: How to Make Models from Paper.* London: Faber and Faber, 1970; New York: St. Martin's Press, 1971. Out of print.

Ward, Tim R. *Paper Aeroplane Pad.* Wargrave, Berkshire, England: John Adams Toys, Ltd., 1977.
    A pad-format book that contains instructions for eight airplanes, pages with pre-marked folding lines, and extra blank sheets. Two models use cutting, and most use staples or paper clips.

Sources

For information on origami, origami activities, and origami societies around the world, send your inquiries, along with a self-addressed envelope with two first class stamps attached, to:

The Friends of the Origami Center of America
15 West 77th St.
New York, NY 10024
(Or call 212-496-1890)

For a source list of origami books and paper which can be ordered by mail, send a self-addressed, stamped envelope to:

The Origami Center of America
Lillian Oppenheimer, Director
31 Union Square West
New York, NY 10003
(Or call 212-255-0469)

For information about the West Coast Origami Guild and its publication, send a self-addressed, stamped envelope to:

Robert Lang
P.O. Box 90601
Pasadena, CA 91109

For information about origami books, paper, activities, and services offered by The British Origami Society, contact:

The British Origami Society
Dave Brill, Honorary Secretary
12 Thorn Road
Bramhall, Stockport
SK7 1HQ England